The Negro Problem

Booker T. Washington
W. E. B. DuBois
Charles W. Chesnutt
Wilford H. Smith
H.T. Kealing
Paul Laurence Dunbar
T. Thomas Fortune

Published by
Seven Treasures Publications
SevenTreasuresPublications@gmail.com
Fax 413-653-8797

Printed in the United States of America

Copyright © 2008   by Seven Treasures Publications

All rights reserved

ISBN 9781440418396

CONTENTS

Industrial Education for the Negro 5
Booker T. Washington

The Talented Tenth 13
W.E. Burghardt DuBois

The Disfranchisement of the Negro 31
Charles W. Chesnutt

The Negro and the Law 49
Wilford H. Smith

The Characteristics of the Negro People 62
H.T. Kealing

Representative American Negroes 71
Paul Laurence Dunbar

The Negro's Place in American Life at the
Present Day 79
T. Thomas Fortune

Industrial Education For The Negro

by BOOKER T. WASHINGTON,
Principal of Tuskegee Institute

The necessity for the race's learning the difference between being worked and working. He would not confine the Negro to industrial life, but believes that the very best service which any one can render to what is called the "higher education" is to teach the present generation to work and save. This will create the wealth from which alone can come leisure and the opportunity for higher education.

One of the most fundamental and far-reaching deeds that has been accomplished during the last quarter of a century has been that by which the Negro has been helped to find himself and to learn the secrets of civilization--to learn that there are a few simple, cardinal principles upon which a race must start its upward course, unless it would fail, and its last estate be worse than its first.

It has been necessary for the Negro to learn the difference between being worked and working--to learn that being worked meant degradation, while working means civilization; that all forms of labor are honorable, and all forms of idleness disgraceful. It has been necessary for him to learn that all races that have got upon their feet have done so largely by laying an economic foundation, and, in general, by beginning in a proper cultivation and ownership of the soil.

Forty years ago my race emerged from slavery into freedom. If, in too many cases, the Negro race began development at the wrong end, it was largely because neither white nor black properly understood the case. Nor is it any wonder that this was so, for never before in the history of the world had just such a problem been presented as that of the two races at the coming of freedom in this country.

For two hundred and fifty years, I believe the way for the redemption of the Negro was being prepared through industrial development. Through all those years the Southern white man did business with the Negro in a way that no one else has done business with him. In most cases if a Southern white man wanted a house built he consulted a Negro mechanic about the plan and about the actual building of the structure. If he wanted a suit of clothes made he went to a Negro tailor, and for shoes he went to a shoemaker of the same race. In a certain way every slave plantation in the South was an industrial school. On these plantations young colored men and women were constantly being trained not only as farmers but as carpenters, blacksmiths, wheelwrights, brick masons, engineers, cooks, laundresses, sewing women and housekeepers.

I do not mean in any way to apologize for the curse of slavery, which was a curse to both races, but in what I say about industrial training in slavery I am simply stating facts. This training was crude, and was given for selfish purposes. It did not answer the highest ends, because there was an absence of mental training in connection with the training of the hand. To a large degree, though, this business contact with the Southern white man, and the industrial training on the plantations, left the Negro at the close of the war in possession of nearly all the common and skilled labor in the South. The industries that gave the South its power, prominence and wealth prior to the Civil War were mainly the raising of cotton, sugar cane, rice and tobacco. Before the way could be prepared for the proper growing and marketing of these crops forests had to be cleared, houses to be built, public roads and railroads constructed. In all these works the Negro did most of the heavy work. In the planting, cultivating and marketing of the crops not only was the Negro the chief dependence, but in the manufacture of tobacco he became a skilled and proficient workman, and in this, up to the present time, in the South, holds the lead in the large tobacco manufactories.

In most of the industries, though, what happened? For nearly twenty years after the war, except in a few instances, the value of the industrial training given by the plantations was overlooked. Negro men and women were educated in literature, in mathematics and in the sciences, with little thought of what had been taking place during the preceding two hundred and fifty years, except, perhaps, as something to be escaped, to be got as far away from as possible. As a generation began to pass, those who had been trained as mechanics in slavery began to disappear by death, and gradually it began to be realized that there were few to take their places. There were young men educated in foreign tongues, but few in carpentry or in mechanical or architectural drawing. Many were trained in Latin, but few as engineers and blacksmiths. Too many were taken from the farm and educated, but educated in everything but farming. For this reason they had no interest in farming and did not return to it. And yet eighty-five per cent. of the Negro population of the Southern states lives and for a considerable time will continue to live in the country districts. The charge is often brought against the members of my race--and too often justly, I confess--that they are found leaving the country districts and flocking into the great cities where temptations are more frequent and harder to resist, and where the Negro people too often become demoralized. Think, though, how frequently it is the case that from the first day that a pupil begins to go to school his books teach him much about the cities of the world and city life, and almost nothing about the country. How natural it is, then, that when he has the ordering of his life he wants to live it in the city.

Only a short time before his death the late Mr. C.P. Huntington, to whose memory a magnificent library has just been given by his widow to the Hampton Institute for Negroes, in Virginia, said in a public address some words which seem to me so wise that I want to quote them here:

"Our schools teach everybody a little of almost everything, but, in my opinion, they teach very few children just what they ought to know in order to make their way successfully in life. They do not put into their hands the tools they are best fitted to use, and hence so many failures. Many a mother and sister have worked and slaved, living upon scanty food, in order to give a son and brother a "liberal education," and in doing this have built up a barrier between the boy and the work he was fitted to do. Let me say to you that all honest work is honorable work. If the labor is manual, and seems common, you will have all the more chance to be thinking of other things, or of work that is higher and brings better pay, and to work out in your minds better and higher duties and responsibilities for yourselves, and for thinking of ways by which you can help others as well as yourselves, and bring them up to your own higher level."

Some years ago, when we decided to make tailoring a part of our training at the Tuskegee Institute, I was amazed to find that it was almost impossible to find in the whole country an educated colored man who could teach the making of clothing. We could find numbers of them who could teach astronomy, theology, Latin or grammar, but almost none who could instruct in the making of clothing, something that has to be used by every one of us every day in the year. How often have I been discouraged as I have gone through the South, and into the homes of the people of my race, and have found women who could converse intelligently upon abstruse subjects, and yet could not tell how to improve the condition of the poorly cooked and still more poorly served bread and meat which they and their families were eating three times a day. It is discouraging to find a girl who can tell you the geographical location of any country on the globe and who does not know where to place the dishes upon a common dinner table. It is discouraging to find a woman who knows much about theoretical chemistry, and who cannot properly wash and iron a shirt.

In what I say here I would not by any means have it understood that I would limit or circumscribe the mental development of the Negro-student. No race can be lifted until its mind is awakened and strengthened. By the side of industrial training should always go mental and moral training, but the pushing of mere abstract knowledge into the head means little. We want more than the mere performance of mental gymnastics. Our knowledge must be harnessed to the things of real life. I would encourage the Negro to secure all the mental strength, all the mental culture--whether gleaned from science, mathematics, history, language or literature that his circumstances will allow, but I believe most earnestly that for years to come the education of the people of my race should be so directed that the greatest proportion of the mental strength of the masses will be brought to bear upon the every-day practical things of life, upon something that is needed to be done, and something which they will be permitted to do in the community in which they reside. And just the same with the professional class which the race needs and must have, I would say give the men and women of that class, too, the training which will best fit them to perform in the most successful manner the service which the race demands.

I would not confine the race to industrial life, not even to agriculture, for example, although I believe that by far the greater part of the Negro race is best off in the country districts and must and should continue to live there, but I would teach the race that in industry the foundation must be laid--that the very best service which any one can render to what is called the higher education is to teach the present generation to provide a material or industrial foundation. On such a foundation as this will grow habits of thrift, a love of work, economy, ownership of property, bank accounts. Out of it in the future will grow practical education, professional education, positions of public responsibility. Out of it will grow moral and religious strength. Out of it will grow wealth from which alone can come leisure and the opportunity for the enjoyment of literature and the fine arts.

In the words of the late beloved Frederick Douglass: "Every blow of the sledge hammer wielded by a sable arm is a powerful blow in support of our cause. Every colored mechanic is by virtue of circumstances an elevator of his race. Every house built by a black man is a strong tower against the allied hosts of prejudice. It is impossible for us to attach too much importance to this aspect of the subject. Without industrial development there can be no wealth; without wealth there can be no leisure; without leisure no opportunity for thoughtful reflection and the cultivation of the higher arts."

I would set no limits to the attainments of the Negro in arts, in letters or statesmanship, but I believe the surest way to reach those ends is by laying the foundation in the little things of life that lie immediately about one's door. I plead for industrial education and development for the Negro not because I want to cramp him, but because I want to free him. I want to see him enter the all-powerful business and commercial world.

It was such combined mental, moral and industrial education which the late General Armstrong set out to give at the Hampton Institute when he established that school thirty years ago. The Hampton Institute has continued along the lines laid down by its great founder, and now each year an increasing number of similar schools are being established in the South, for the people of both races.

Early in the history of the Tuskegee Institute we began to combine industrial training with mental and moral culture. Our first efforts were in the direction of agriculture, and we began teaching this with no appliances except one hoe and a blind mule. From this small beginning we have grown until now the Institute owns two thousand acres of land, eight hundred of which are cultivated each year by the young men of the school. We began teaching wheelwrighting and blacksmithing in a small way to the men, and laundry work, cooking and sewing and housekeeping to the young women. The fourteen hundred and over young men and women who attended the school during the last school year received instruction--in addition to academic and religious training--in thirty-three trades and industries, including carpentry, blacksmithing, printing, wheelwrighting harnessmaking, painting, machinery, founding, shoemaking, brickmasonry and brickmaking, plastering, sawmilling, tinsmithing, tailoring, mechanical and architectural drawing, electrical and steam engineering, canning, sewing, dressmaking, millinery, cooking, laundering, housekeeping, mattress making, basketry, nursing, agriculture, dairying and stock raising, horticulture.

Not only do the students receive instruction in these trades, but they do actual work, by means of which more than half of them pay some part or all of their expenses while remaining at the school. Of the sixty buildings belonging to the school all but four were almost wholly erected by the students as a part of their industrial education.

Even the bricks which go into the walls are made by students in the school's brick yard, in which, last year, they manufactured two million bricks.

When we first began this work at Tuskegee, and the idea got spread among the people of my race that the students who came to the Tuskegee school were to be taught industries in connection with their academic studies, were, in other words, to be taught to work, I received a great many verbal messages and letters from parents informing me that they wanted their children taught books, but not how to work. This protest went on for three or four years, but I am glad to be able to say now that our people have very generally been educated to a point where they see their own needs and conditions so clearly that it has been several years since we have had a single protest from parents against the teaching of industries, and there is now a positive enthusiasm for it. In fact, public sentiment among the students at Tuskegee is now so strong for industrial training that it would hardly permit a student to remain on the grounds who was unwilling to labor.

It seems to me that too often mere book education leaves the Negro young man or woman in a weak position. For example, I have seen a Negro girl taught by her mother to help her in doing laundry work at home. Later, when this same girl was graduated from the public schools or a high school and returned home she finds herself educated out of sympathy with laundry work, and yet not able to find anything to do which seems in keeping with the cost and character of her education. Under these circumstances we cannot be surprised if she does not fulfill the expectations made for her. What should have been done for her, it seems to me, was to give her along with her academic education thorough training in the latest and best methods of laundry work, so that she could have put so much skill and intelligence into it that the work would have been lifted out from the plane of drudgery[A]. The home which she would then have been able to found by the results of her work would have enabled her to help her children to take a still more responsible position in life.

Almost from the first Tuskegee has kept in mind--and this I think should be the policy of all industrial schools--fitting students for occupations which would be open to them in their home communities. Some years ago we noted the fact that there was beginning to be a demand in the South for men to operate dairies in a skillful, modern manner. We opened a dairy department in connection with the school, where a number of young men could have instruction in the latest and most scientific methods of dairy work. At present we have calls--mainly from Southern white men--

for twice as many dairymen as we are able to supply. What is equally satisfactory, the reports which come to us indicate that our young men are giving the highest satisfaction and are fast changing and improving the dairy product in the communities into which they go. I use the dairy here as an example. What I have said of this is equally true of many of the other industries which we teach. Aside from the economic value of this work I cannot but believe, and my observation confirms me in my belief, that as we continue to place Negro men and women of intelligence, religion, modesty, conscience and skill in every community in the South, who will prove by actual results their value to the community, I cannot but believe, I say, that this will constitute a solution to many of the present political and social difficulties.

Many seem to think that industrial education is meant to make the Negro work as he worked in the days of slavery. This is far from my conception of industrial education. If this training is worth anything to the Negro, it consists in teaching him how not to work, but how to make the forces of nature--air, steam, water, horse-power and electricity--work for him. If it has any value it is in lifting labor up out of toil and drudgery into the plane of the dignified and the beautiful. The Negro in the South works and works hard; but too often his ignorance and lack of skill causes him to do his work in the most costly and shiftless manner, and this keeps him near the bottom of the ladder in the economic world.

I have not emphasized particularly in these pages the great need of training the Negro in agriculture, but I believe that this branch of industrial education does need very great emphasis. In this connection I want to quote some words which Mr. Edgar Gardner Murphy, of Montgomery, Alabama, has recently written upon this subject:

"We must incorporate into our public school system a larger recognition of the practical and industrial elements in educational training. Ours is an agricultural population. The school must be brought more closely to the soil. The teaching of history, for example, is all very well, but nobody can really know anything of history unless he has been taught to see things grow--has so seen things not only with the outward eye, but with the eyes of his intelligence and conscience. The actual things of the present are more important, however, than the institutions of the past. Even to young children can be shown the simpler conditions and processes of growth--how corn is put into the ground--how cotton and potatoes should be planted--how to choose the soil best adapted to a particular plant, how to improve that soil, how to care for the plant while it grows, how to get the most value out of it, how to use the elements of waste for the fertilization of other crops; how, through the alternation of crops, the land may be made to increase the annual value of its products--these things, upon their elementary side are absolutely vital to the worth and success of hundreds of thousands of these people of the Negro race, and yet our whole educational system has practically ignored them.

* * * * *

"Such work will mean not only an education in agriculture, but an education through agriculture and education, through natural symbols and practical forms, which will educate as deeply, as broadly and as truly as any other system which the world has known. Such changes will bring far larger results than the mere improvement of our Negroes. They will give us an agricultural class, a class of tenants or small land owners, trained not away from the soil, but in relation to the soil and in intelligent dependence upon its resources."

I close, then, as I began, by saying that as a slave the Negro was worked, and that as a freeman he must learn to work. There is still doubt in many quarters as to the ability of the Negro unguided, unsupported, to hew his own path and put into visible, tangible, indisputable form, products and signs of civilization. This doubt cannot be much affected by abstract arguments, no matter how delicately and convincingly woven together. Patiently, quietly, doggedly, persistently, through summer and winter, sunshine and shadow, by self-sacrifice, by foresight, by honesty and industry, we must re-enforce argument with results. One farm bought, one house built, one home sweetly and intelligently kept, one man who is the largest tax payer or has the largest bank account, one school or church maintained, one factory running successfully, one truck garden profitably cultivated, one patient cured by a Negro doctor, one sermon well preached, one office well filled, one life cleanly lived--these will tell more in our favor than all the abstract eloquence that can be summoned to plead our cause. Our pathway must be up through the soil, up through swamps, up through forests, up through the streams, the rocks, up through commerce, education and religion!

The Talented Tenth

by PROF. W.E. BURGHARDT DuBOIS

A strong plea for the higher education of the Negro, which those who are interested in the future of the freedmen cannot afford to ignore. Prof. DuBois produces ample evidence to prove conclusively the truth of his statement that "to attempt to establish any sort of a system of common and industrial school training, without first providing for the higher training of the very best teachers, is simply throwing your money to the winds."

The Negro race, like all races, is going to be saved by its exceptional men. The problem of education, then, among Negroes must first of all deal with the Talented Tenth; it is the problem of developing the Best of this race that they may guide the Mass away from the contamination and death of the Worst, in their own and other races. Now the training of men is a difficult and intricate task. Its technique is a matter for educational experts, but its object is for the vision of seers. If we make money the object of man-training, we shall develop money-makers but not necessarily men; if we make technical skill the object of education, we may possess artisans but not, in nature, men. Men we shall have only as we make manhood the object of the work of the schools--intelligence, broad sympathy, knowledge of the world that was and is, and of the relation of men to it--this is the curriculum of that Higher Education which must underlie true life. On this foundation we may build bread winning, skill of hand and quickness of brain, with never a fear lest the child and man mistake the means of living for the object of life.

* * * * *

If this be true--and who can deny it--three tasks lay before me; first to show from the past that the Talented Tenth as they have risen among American Negroes have been worthy of leadership; secondly, to show how these men may be educated and developed; and thirdly, to show their relation to the Negro problem.

* * * * *

You misjudge us because you do not know us. From the very first it has been the educated and intelligent of the Negro people that have led and elevated the mass, and the sole obstacles that nullified and retarded their efforts were slavery and race prejudice; for what is slavery but the legalized survival of the unfit and the nullification of the work of natural internal leadership? Negro leadership, therefore, sought from the first to rid the race of this awful incubus that it might make way for natural selection and the survival of the fittest. In colonial days came Phillis Wheatley and Paul Cuffe striving against the bars of prejudice; and Benjamin Banneker, the almanac maker, voiced their longings when he said to Thomas Jefferson, "I freely and cheerfully acknowledge that I am of the African race, and in colour which is natural to them, of the deepest dye; and it is under a sense of the most profound gratitude to the Supreme Ruler of the Universe, that I now confess to you that I am not under that state of tyrannical thraldom and inhuman captivity to which too many of my brethren are doomed, but that I have abundantly tasted of the fruition of those blessings which proceed from that free and unequalled liberty with which you are favored, and which I hope you will willingly allow, you have mercifully received from the immediate hand of that Being from whom proceedeth every good and perfect gift.

"Suffer me to recall to your mind that time, in which the arms of the British crown were exerted with every powerful effort, in order to reduce you to a state of servitude; look back, I entreat you, on the variety of dangers to which you were exposed; reflect on that period in which every human aid appeared unavailable, and in which even hope and fortitude wore the aspect of inability to the conflict, and you cannot but be led to a serious and grateful sense of your miraculous and providential preservation, you cannot but acknowledge, that the present freedom and tranquility which you enjoy, you have mercifully received, and that a peculiar blessing of heaven.

"This, sir, was a time when you clearly saw into the injustice of a state of Slavery, and in which you had just apprehensions of the horrors of its condition. It was then that your abhorrence thereof was so excited, that you publicly held forth this true and invaluable doctrine, which is worthy to be recorded and remembered in all succeeding ages: 'We hold these truths to be self evident, that all men are created equal; that they are endowed with certain inalienable rights, and that among these are life, liberty and the pursuit of happiness.'"

Then came Dr. James Derham, who could tell even the learned Dr. Rush something of medicine, and Lemuel Haynes, to whom Middlebury College gave an honorary A.M. in 1804. These and others we may call the Revolutionary group of distinguished Negroes--they were persons of marked ability, leaders of a Talented Tenth, standing conspicuously among the best of their time. They strove by word and deed to save the color line from becoming the line between the bond and free, but all they could do was nullified by Eli Whitney and the Curse of Gold. So they passed into forgetfulness.

But their spirit did not wholly die; here and there in the early part of the century came other exceptional men. Some were natural sons of unnatural fathers and were given often a liberal training and thus a race of educated mulattoes sprang up to plead for black men's rights. There was Ira Aldridge, whom all Europe loved to honor; there was that Voice crying in the Wilderness, David Walker, and saying:

"I declare it does appear to me as though some nations think God is asleep, or that he made the Africans for nothing else but to dig their mines and work their farms, or they cannot believe history, sacred or profane. I ask every man who has a heart, and is blessed with the privilege of believing--Is not God a God of justice to all his creatures? Do you say he is? Then if he gives peace and tranquility to tyrants and permits them to keep our fathers, our mothers, ourselves and our children in eternal ignorance and wretchedness to support them and their families, would he be to us a God of Justice? I ask, O, ye Christians, who hold us and our children in the most abject ignorance and degradation that ever a people were afflicted with since the world began--I say if God gives you peace and tranquility, and suffers you thus to go on afflicting us, and our children, who have never given you the least provocation--would He be to us a God of Justice? If you will allow that we are men, who feel for each other, does not the blood of our fathers and of us, their children, cry aloud to the Lord of Sabaoth against you for the cruelties and murders with which you have and do continue to afflict us?"

This was the wild voice that first aroused Southern legislators in 1829 to the terrors of abolitionism.

In 1831 there met that first Negro convention in Philadelphia, at which the world gaped curiously but which bravely attacked the problems of race and slavery, crying out against persecution and declaring that "Laws as cruel in themselves as they were unconstitutional and unjust, have in many places been enacted against our poor, unfriended and unoffending brethren (without a shadow of provocation on our part), at whose bare recital the very savage draws himself up for fear of contagion--looks noble and prides himself because he bears not the name of Christian." Side by side this free Negro movement, and the movement for abolition, strove until they merged into one strong stream. Too little notice has been taken of the work which the Talented Tenth among Negroes took in the great abolition crusade. From the very day that a Philadelphia colored man became the first subscriber to Garrison's "Liberator," to the day when Negro soldiers made the Emancipation Proclamation possible, black leaders worked shoulder to shoulder with white men in a movement, the success of which would have been impossible without them. There was Purvis and Remond, Pennington and Highland Garnett, Sojourner Truth and Alexander Crummel, and above all, Frederick Douglass--what would the abolition movement have been without them? They stood as living examples of the possibilities of the Negro race, their own hard experiences and well wrought culture said silently more than all the drawn periods of orators--they were the men who made American slavery impossible. As Maria Weston Chapman once said, from the school of anti-slavery agitation "a throng of authors, editors, lawyers, orators and accomplished gentlemen of color have taken their degree! It has equally implanted hopes and aspirations, noble thoughts, and sublime purposes, in the hearts of both races. It has prepared the white man for the freedom of the black man, and it has made the black man scorn the thought of enslavement, as does a white man, as far as its influence has extended. Strengthen that noble influence! Before its organization, the country only saw here and there in slavery some faithful Cudjoe or Dinah, whose strong natures blossomed even in bondage, like a fine plant beneath a heavy stone. Now, under the elevating and cherishing influence of the American Anti-slavery Society, the colored race, like the white, furnishes Corinthian capitals for the noblest temples."

Where were these black abolitionists trained? Some, like Frederick Douglass, were self-trained, but yet trained liberally; others, like Alexander Crummell and McCune Smith, graduated from famous foreign universities. Most of them rose up through the colored schools of New York and Philadelphia and Boston, taught by college-bred men like Russworm, of Dartmouth, and college-bred white men like Neau and Benezet.

After emancipation came a new group of educated and gifted leaders: Langston, Bruce and Elliot, Greener, Williams and Payne. Through political organization, historical and polemic writing and moral regeneration, these men strove to uplift their people. It is the fashion of to-day to sneer at them and to say that with freedom Negro leadership should have begun at the plow and not in the Senate--a foolish and mischievous lie; two hundred and fifty years that black serf toiled at the plow and yet that toiling was in vain till the Senate passed the war amendments; and two hundred and fifty years more the half-free serf of to-day may toil at his plow, but unless he have political rights and righteously guarded civic status, he will still remain the poverty-stricken and ignorant plaything of rascals, that he now is. This all sane men know even if they dare not say it.

And so we come to the present--a day of cowardice and vacillation, of strident wide-voiced wrong and faint hearted compromise; of double-faced dallying with Truth and Right. Who are to-day guiding the work of the Negro people? The "exceptions" of course. And yet so sure as this Talented Tenth is pointed out, the blind worshippers of the Average cry out in alarm: "These are exceptions, look here at death, disease and crime--these are the happy rule." Of course they are the rule, because a silly nation made them the rule: Because for three long centuries this people lynched Negroes who dared to be brave, raped black women who dared to be virtuous, crushed dark-hued youth who dared to be ambitious, and encouraged and made to flourish servility and lewdness and apathy. But not even this was able to crush all manhood and chastity and aspiration from black folk. A saving remnant continually survives and persists, continually aspires, continually shows itself in thrift and ability and character. Exceptional it is to be sure, but this is its chiefest promise; it shows the capability of Negro blood, the promise of black men. Do Americans ever stop to reflect that there are in this land a million men of Negro blood, well-educated, owners of homes, against the honor of whose womanhood no breath was ever raised, whose men occupy positions of trust and usefulness, and who, judged by any standard, have reached the full measure of the best type of modern European culture? Is it fair, is it decent, is it Christian to ignore these facts of the Negro problem, to belittle such aspiration, to nullify such leadership and seek to crush these people back into the mass out of which by toil and travail, they and their fathers have raised themselves?

Can the masses of the Negro people be in any possible way more quickly raised than by the effort and example of this aristocracy of talent and character? Was there ever a nation on God's fair earth civilized from the bottom upward? Never; it is, ever was and ever will be from the top downward that culture filters. The Talented Tenth rises and pulls all that are worth the saving up to their vantage ground. This is the history of human progress; and the two historic mistakes which have hindered that progress were the thinking first that no more could ever rise save the few already risen; or second, that it would better the unrisen to pull the risen down.

How then shall the leaders of a struggling people be trained and the hands of the risen few strengthened? There can be but one answer: The best and most capable of their youth must be schooled in the colleges and universities of the land. We will not quarrel as to just what the university of the Negro should teach or how it should teach it--I willingly admit that each soul and each race-soul needs its own peculiar curriculum. But this is true: A university is a human invention for the transmission of knowledge and culture from generation to generation, through the training of quick minds and pure hearts, and for this work no other human invention will suffice, not even trade and industrial schools.

All men cannot go to college but some men must; every isolated group or nation must have its yeast, must have for the talented few centers of training where men are not so mystified and befuddled by the hard and necessary toil of earning a living, as to have no aims higher than their bellies, and no God greater than Gold. This is true training, and thus in the beginning were the favored sons of the freedmen trained. Out of the colleges of the North came, after the blood of war, Ware, Cravath, Chase, Andrews, Bumstead and Spence to build the foundations of knowledge and civilization in the black South. Where ought they to have begun to build? At the bottom, of course, quibbles the mole with his eyes in the earth. Aye! truly at the bottom, at the very bottom; at the bottom of knowledge, down in the very depths of knowledge there where the roots of justice strike into the lowest soil of Truth. And so they did begin; they founded colleges, and up from the colleges shot normal schools, and out from the normal schools went teachers, and around the normal teachers clustered other teachers to teach the public schools; the college trained in Greek and Latin and mathematics, 2,000 men; and these men trained full 50,000 others in morals and manners, and they in turn taught thrift and the alphabet to nine millions of men, who to-day hold $300,000,000 of property. It was a miracle--the most wonderful peace-battle of the 19th century, and yet to-day men smile at it, and in fine superiority tell us that it was all a strange mistake; that a proper way to found a system of education is first to gather the children and buy them spelling books and hoes; afterward men may look about for teachers, if haply they may find them; or again they would teach men Work, but as for Life--why, what has Work to do with Life, they ask vacantly.

Was the work of these college founders successful; did it stand the test of time? Did the college graduates, with all their fine theories of life, really live? Are they useful men helping to civilize and elevate their less fortunate fellows? Let us see. Omitting all institutions which have not actually graduated students from a college course, there are to-day in the United States thirty-four institutions giving something above high school training to Negroes and designed especially for this race.

Three of these were established in border States before the War; thirteen were planted by the Freedmen's Bureau in the years 1864-1869; nine were established between 1870 and 1880 by various church bodies; five were established after 1881 by Negro churches, and four are state institutions supported by United States' agricultural funds. In most cases the college departments are small adjuncts to high and common school work. As a matter of fact six institutions--Atlanta, Fisk, Howard, Shaw, Wilberforce and Leland, are the important Negro colleges so far as actual work and number of students are concerned. In all these institutions, seven hundred and fifty Negro college students are enrolled. In grade the best of these colleges are about a year behind the smaller New England colleges and a typical curriculum is that of Atlanta University. Here students from the grammar grades, after a three years' high school course, take a college course of 136 weeks. One-fourth of this time is given to Latin and Greek; one-fifth, to English and modern languages; one-sixth, to history and social science; one-seventh, to natural science; one-eighth to mathematics, and one-eighth to philosophy and pedagogy.

In addition to these students in the South, Negroes have attended Northern colleges for many years. As early as 1826 one was graduated from Bowdoin College, and from that time till to-day nearly every year has seen elsewhere, other such graduates. They have, of course, met much color prejudice. Fifty years ago very few colleges would admit them at all. Even to-day no Negro has ever been admitted to Princeton, and at some other leading institutions they are rather endured than encouraged. Oberlin was the great pioneer in the work of blotting out the color line in colleges, and has more Negro graduates by far than any other Northern college.

The total number of Negro college graduates up to 1899, (several of the graduates of that year not being reported), was as follows:

	Negro Colleges	White Colleges
Before '76	137	75
'75-80	143	22
'80-85	250	31
'85-90	413	43
'90-95	465	66
'96-99	475	88
Class Unknown	57	64
Total	1,914	390

Of these graduates 2,079 were men and 252 were women; 50 per cent. of Northern-born college men come South to work among the masses of their people, at a sacrifice which few people realize; nearly 90 per cent. of the Southern-born graduates instead of seeking that personal freedom and broader intellectual atmosphere which their training has led them, in some degree, to conceive, stay and labor and wait in the midst of their black neighbors and relatives.

The most interesting question, and in many respects the crucial question, to be asked concerning college-bred Negroes, is: Do they earn a living? It has been intimated more than once that the higher training of Negroes has resulted in sending into the world of work, men who could find nothing to do suitable to their talents. Now and then there comes a rumor of a colored college man working at menial service, etc. Fortunately, returns as to occupations of college-bred Negroes, gathered by the Atlanta conference, are quite full-- nearly sixty per cent. of the total number of graduates.

This enables us to reach fairly certain conclusions as to the occupations of all college-bred Negroes. Of 1,312 persons reported, there were:

	Per Cent
Teachers	53.4
Clergymen	16.8
Physicians, etc.	6.3
Students	5.6
Lawyers	4.7
In Govt. Service	4.0
In Business	3.6
Farmers and Artisans	2.7
Editors, Secretaries and Clerks	2.4
Miscellaneous	.5

Over half are teachers, a sixth are preachers, another sixth are students and professional men; over 6 per cent. are farmers, artisans and merchants, and 4 per cent. are in government service. In detail the occupations are as follows:

Occupations of College-Bred Men.

Teachers:		
Presidents and Deans,	19	
Teacher of Music	7	
Professors, Principals and Teachers	675	Total 701
Clergymen:		
Bishop	1	
Chaplains U.S. Army	2	
Missionaries		
Presiding Elders	12	
Preachers	197	Total 221
Physicians,		
Doctors of Medicine	76	
Druggists	4	
Dentists	3	Total 83
Students	74	
Lawyers	62	
Civil Service:		
U.S. Minister Plenipotentiary	1	
U.S. Consul	1	
U.S. Deputy Collector	1	
U.S. Gauger	1	
U.S. Postmasters	2	
U.S. Clerks	44	
State Civil Service	2	
City Civil Service	1	Total 53
Business Men:		
Merchants, etc.	30	
Managers	13	
Real Estate Dealers	4	Total 47
Farmers	26	

Clerks and Secretaries:		
Secretary of National Societies	7	
Clerks, etc.	15	Total 22
Artisans	9	
Editors	9	
Miscellaneous	5	

These figures illustrate vividly the function of the college-bred Negro. He is, as he ought to be, the group leader, the man who sets the ideals of the community where he lives, directs its thoughts and heads its social movements. It need hardly be argued that the Negro people need social leadership more than most groups; that they have no traditions to fall back upon, no long established customs, no strong family ties, no well defined social classes. All these things must be slowly and painfully evolved. The preacher was, even before the war, the group leader of the Negroes, and the church their greatest social institution. Naturally this preacher was ignorant and often immoral, and the problem of replacing the older type by better educated men has been a difficult one. Both by direct work and by direct influence on other preachers, and on congregations, the college-bred preacher has an opportunity for reformatory work and moral inspiration, the value of which cannot be overestimated.

It has, however, been in the furnishing of teachers that the Negro college has found its peculiar function. Few persons realize how vast a work, how mighty a revolution has been thus accomplished. To furnish five millions and more of ignorant people with teachers of their own race and blood, in one generation, was not only a very difficult undertaking, but a very important one, in that, it placed before the eyes of almost every Negro child an attainable ideal. It brought the masses of the blacks in contact with modern civilization, made black men the leaders of their communities and trainers of the new generation. In this work college-bred Negroes were first teachers, and then teachers of teachers. And here it is that the broad culture of college work has been of peculiar value. Knowledge of life and its wider meaning, has been the point of the Negro's deepest ignorance, and the sending out of teachers whose training has not been simply for bread winning, but also for human culture, has been of inestimable value in the training of these men.

In earlier years the two occupations of preacher and teacher were practically the only ones open to the black college graduate. Of later years a larger diversity of life among his people, has opened new avenues of employment. Nor have these college men been paupers and spendthrifts; 557 college-bred Negroes owned in 1899, $1,342,862.50 worth of real estate, (assessed value) or $2,411 per family. The real value of the total accumulations of the whole group is perhaps about $10,000,000, or $5,000 a piece. Pitiful, is it not, beside the fortunes of oil kings and steel trusts, but after all is the fortune of the millionaire the only stamp of true and successful living? Alas! it is, with many, and there's the rub.

The problem of training the Negro is to-day immensely complicated by the fact that the whole question of the efficiency and appropriateness of our present systems of education, for any kind of child, is a matter of active debate, in which final settlement seems still afar off. Consequently it often happens that persons arguing for or against certain systems of education for Negroes, have these controversies in mind and miss the real question at issue. The main question, so far as the Southern Negro is concerned, is: What under the present circumstance, must a system of education do in order to raise the Negro as quickly as possible in the scale of civilization? The answer to this question seems to me clear: It must strengthen the Negro's character, increase his knowledge and teach him to earn a living. Now it goes without saying, that it is hard to do all these things simultaneously or suddenly, and that at the same time it will not do to give all the attention to one and neglect the others; we could give black boys trades, but that alone will not civilize a race of ex-slaves; we might simply increase their knowledge of the world, but this would not necessarily make them wish to use this knowledge honestly; we might seek to strengthen character and purpose, but to what end if this people have nothing to eat or to wear? A system of education is not one thing, nor does it have a single definite object, nor is it a mere matter of schools. Education is that whole system of human training within and without the school house walls, which molds and develops men. If then we start out to train an ignorant and unskilled people with a heritage of bad habits, our system of training must set before itself two great aims--the one dealing with knowledge and character, the other part seeking to give the child the technical knowledge necessary for him to earn a living under the present circumstances. These objects are accomplished in part by the opening of the common schools on the one, and of the industrial schools on the other. But only in part, for there must also be trained those who are to teach these schools--men and women of knowledge and culture and technical skill who understand modern civilization, and have the training and aptitude to impart it to the children under them. There must be teachers, and teachers of teachers, and to attempt to establish any sort of a system of common and industrial school training, without first (and I say first advisedly) without first providing for the higher training of the very best teachers, is simply throwing your money to the winds. School houses do not teach themselves--piles of brick and mortar and machinery do not send out men . It is the trained, living human soul, cultivated and strengthened by long study and thought, that breathes the real breath of life into boys and girls and makes them human, whether they be black or white, Greek, Russian or American. Nothing, in these latter days, has so dampened the faith of thinking Negroes in recent educational movements, as the fact that such movements have been accompanied by ridicule and denouncement and decrying of those very institutions of higher training which made the Negro public school possible, and make Negro industrial schools thinkable. It was Fisk, Atlanta, Howard and Straight, those colleges born of the faith and sacrifice of the abolitionists, that placed in the black schools of the South the 30,000 teachers and more, which some, who depreciate the work of these higher schools, are using to teach their own new experiments. If Hampton, Tuskegee and the hundred other industrial schools prove in the future to be as successful as they deserve to be, then their success in training black artisans for the South, will be due primarily to the white colleges of the North and the black colleges of the South, which trained the teachers who to-day conduct these institutions. There was a time when the American people believed pretty devoutly that a log of wood with a boy at one end and Mark Hopkins at the other, represented the highest ideal of human training. But in these eager days it would seem that we have changed all that and think it necessary to add a couple of saw-mills and a hammer to this outfit, and, at a pinch, to dispense with the services of Mark Hopkins.

 I would not deny, or for a moment seem to deny, the paramount necessity of teaching the Negro to work, and to work steadily and skillfully; or seem to depreciate in the slightest degree the important part industrial schools must play in the accomplishment of these ends, but I do say, and insist upon it, that it is industrialism drunk with its vision of success, to imagine that its own work can be accomplished without providing for the training of broadly cultured men and women to teach its own teachers, and to teach the teachers of the public schools.

But I have already said that human education is not simply a matter of schools; it is much more a matter of family and group life-- the training of one's home, of one's daily companions, of one's social class. Now the black boy of the South moves in a black world--a world with its own leaders, its own thoughts, its own ideals. In this world he gets by far the larger part of his life training, and through the eyes of this dark world he peers into the veiled world beyond. Who guides and determines the education which he receives in his world? His teachers here are the group-leaders of the Negro people-- the physicians and clergymen, the trained fathers and mothers, the influential and forceful men about him of all kinds; here it is, if at all, that the culture of the surrounding world trickles through and is handed on by the graduates of the higher schools. Can such culture training of group leaders be neglected? Can we afford to ignore it? Do you think that if the leaders of thought among Negroes are not trained and educated thinkers, that they will have no leaders? On the contrary a hundred half-trained demagogues will still hold the places they so largely occupy now, and hundreds of vociferous busy-bodies will multiply. You have no choice; either you must help furnish this race from within its own ranks with thoughtful men of trained leadership, or you must suffer the evil consequences of a headless misguided rabble.

I am an earnest advocate of manual training and trade teaching for black boys, and for white boys, too. I believe that next to the founding of Negro colleges the most valuable addition to Negro education since the war, has been industrial training for black boys. Nevertheless, I insist that the object of all true education is not to make men carpenters, it is to make carpenters men; there are two means of making the carpenter a man, each equally important: the first is to give the group and community in which he works, liberally trained teachers and leaders to teach him and his family what life means; the second is to give him sufficient intelligence and technical skill to make him an efficient workman; the first object demands the Negro college and college-bred men--not a quantity of such colleges, but a few of excellent quality; not too many college-bred men, but enough to leaven the lump, to inspire the masses, to raise the Talented Tenth to leadership; the second object demands a good system of common schools, well-taught, conveniently located and properly equipped.

The Sixth Atlanta Conference truly said in 1901:

"We call the attention of the Nation to the fact that less than one million of the three million Negro children of school age, are at present regularly attending school, and these attend a session which lasts only a few months.

"We are to-day deliberately rearing millions of our citizens in ignorance, and at the same time limiting the rights of citizenship by educational qualifications. This is unjust. Half the black youth of the land have no opportunities open to them for learning to read, write and cipher. In the discussion as to the proper training of Negro children after they leave the public schools, we have forgotten that they are not yet decently provided with public schools.

"Propositions are beginning to be made in the South to reduce the already meager school facilities of Negroes. We congratulate the South on resisting, as much as it has, this pressure, and on the many millions it has spent on Negro education. But it is only fair to point out that Negro taxes and the Negroes' share of the income from indirect taxes and endowments have fully repaid this expenditure, so that the Negro public school system has not in all probability cost the white taxpayers a single cent since the war.

"This is not fair. Negro schools should be a public burden, since they are a public benefit. The Negro has a right to demand good common school training at the hands of the States and the Nation since by their fault he is not in position to pay for this himself."

What is the chief need for the building up of the Negro public school in the South? The Negro race in the South needs teachers to-day above all else. This is the concurrent testimony of all who know the situation. For the supply of this great demand two things are needed--institutions of higher education and money for school houses and salaries. It is usually assumed that a hundred or more institutions for Negro training are to-day turning out so many teachers and college-bred men that the race is threatened with an over-supply. This is sheer nonsense. There are to-day less than 3,000 living Negro college graduates in the United States, and less than 1,000 Negroes in college. Moreover, in the 164 schools for Negroes, 95 per cent. of their students are doing elementary and secondary work, work which should be done in the public schools. Over half the remaining 2,157 students are taking high school studies. The mass of so-called "normal" schools for the Negro, are simply doing elementary common school work, or, at most, high school work, with a little instruction in methods. The Negro colleges and the post-graduate courses at other institutions are the only agencies for the broader and more careful training of teachers. The work of these institutions is hampered for lack of funds. It is getting increasingly difficult to get funds for training teachers in the best modern methods, and yet all over the South, from State Superintendents, county officials, city boards and school principals comes the wail, "We need TEACHERS!" and teachers must be trained. As the fairest minded of all white Southerners, Atticus G. Haygood, once said: "The defects of colored teachers are so great as to create an urgent necessity for training better ones. Their excellencies and their successes are sufficient to justify the best hopes of success in the effort, and to vindicate the judgment of those who make large investments of money and service, to give to colored students opportunity for thoroughly preparing themselves for the work of teaching children of their people."

The truth of this has been strikingly shown in the marked improvement of white teachers in the South. Twenty years ago the rank and file of white public school teachers were not as good as the Negro teachers. But they, by scholarships and good salaries, have been encouraged to thorough normal and collegiate preparation, while the Negro teachers have been discouraged by starvation wages and the idea that any training will do for a black teacher. If carpenters are needed it is well and good to train men as carpenters. But to train men as carpenters, and then set them to teaching is wasteful and criminal; and to train men as teachers and then refuse them living wages, unless they become carpenters, is rank nonsense.

The United States Commissioner of Education says in his report for 1900: "For comparison between the white and colored enrollment in secondary and higher education, I have added together the enrollment in high schools and secondary schools, with the attendance on colleges and universities, not being sure of the actual grade of work done in the colleges and universities. The work done in the secondary schools is reported in such detail in this office, that there can be no doubt of its grade."

He then makes the following comparisons of persons in every million enrolled in secondary and higher education:

	Whole Country	Negroes
1880	4,362	1,289
1900	10,743	2,061

And he concludes: "While the number in colored high schools and colleges had increased somewhat faster than the population, it had not kept pace with the average of the whole country, for it had fallen from 30 per cent. to 24 per cent. of the average quota. Of all colored pupils, one (1) in one hundred was engaged in secondary and higher work, and that ratio has continued substantially for the past twenty years. If the ratio of colored population in secondary and higher education is to be equal to the average for the whole country, it must be increased to five times its present average." And if this be true of the secondary and higher education, it is safe to say that the Negro has not one-tenth his quota in college studies. How baseless, therefore, is the charge of too much training! We need Negro teachers for the Negro common schools, and we need first-class normal schools and colleges to train them. This is the work of higher Negro education and it must be done.

Further than this, after being provided with group leaders of civilization, and a foundation of intelligence in the public schools, the carpenter, in order to be a man, needs technical skill. This calls for trade schools. Now trade schools are not nearly such simple things as people once thought. The original idea was that the "Industrial" school was to furnish education, practically free, to those willing to work for it; it was to "do" things--i.e.: become a center of productive industry, it was to be partially, if not wholly, self-supporting, and it was to teach trades. Admirable as were some of the ideas underlying this scheme, the whole thing simply would not work in practice; it was found that if you were to use time and material to teach trades thoroughly, you could not at the same time keep the industries on a commercial basis and make them pay. Many schools started out to do this on a large scale and went into virtual bankruptcy. Moreover, it was found also that it was possible to teach a boy a trade mechanically, without giving him the full educative benefit of the process, and, vice versa, that there was a distinctive educative value in teaching a boy to use his hands and eyes in carrying out certain physical processes, even though he did not actually learn a trade. It has happened, therefore, in the last decade, that a noticeable change has come over the industrial schools. In the first place the idea of commercially remunerative industry in a school is being pushed rapidly to the back-ground. There are still schools with shops and farms that bring an income, and schools that use student labor partially for the erection of their buildings and the furnishing of equipment. It is coming to be seen, however, in the education of the Negro, as clearly as it has been seen in the education of the youths the world over, that it is the boy and not the material product, that is the true object of education. Consequently the object of the industrial school came to be the thorough training of boys regardless of the cost of the training, so long as it was thoroughly well done.

Even at this point, however, the difficulties were not surmounted. In the first place modern industry has taken great strides since the war, and the teaching of trades is no longer a simple matter. Machinery and long processes of work have greatly changed the work of the carpenter, the ironworker and the shoemaker. A really efficient workman must be to-day an intelligent man who has had good technical training in addition to thorough common school, and perhaps even higher training. To meet this situation the industrial schools began a further development; they established distinct Trade Schools for the thorough training of better class artisans, and at the same time they sought to preserve for the purposes of general education, such of the simpler processes of elementary trade learning as were best suited therefor. In this differentiation of the Trade School and manual training, the best of the industrial schools simply followed the plain trend of the present educational epoch. A prominent educator tells us that, in Sweden, "In the beginning the economic conception was generally adopted, and everywhere manual training was looked upon as a means of preparing the children of the common people to earn their living. But gradually it came to be recognized that manual training has a more elevated purpose, and one, indeed, more useful in the deeper meaning of the term. It came to be considered as an educative process for the complete moral, physical and intellectual development of the child."

Thus, again, in the manning of trade schools and manual training schools we are thrown back upon the higher training as its source and chief support. There was a time when any aged and wornout carpenter could teach in a trade school. But not so to-day. Indeed the demand for college-bred men by a school like Tuskegee, ought to make Mr. Booker T. Washington the firmest friend of higher training. Here he has as helpers the son of a Negro senator, trained in Greek and the humanities, and graduated at Harvard; the son of a Negro congressman and lawyer, trained in Latin and mathematics, and graduated at Oberlin; he has as his wife, a woman who read Virgil and Homer in the same class room with me; he has as college chaplain, a classical graduate of Atlanta University; as teacher of science, a graduate of Fisk; as teacher of history, a graduate of Smith,--indeed some thirty of his chief teachers are college graduates, and instead of studying French grammars in the midst of weeds, or buying pianos for dirty cabins, they are at Mr. Washington's right hand helping him in a noble work. And yet one of the effects of Mr. Washington's propaganda has been to throw doubt upon the expediency of such training for Negroes, as these persons have had.

* * * * *

Men of America, the problem is plain before you. Here is a race transplanted through the criminal foolishness of your fathers. Whether you like it or not the millions are here, and here they will remain. If you do not lift them up, they will pull you down. Education and work are the levers to uplift a people. Work alone will not do it unless inspired by the right ideals and guided by intelligence. Education must not simply teach work--it must teach Life. The Talented Tenth of the Negro race must be made leaders of thought and missionaries of culture among their people. No others can do this work and Negro colleges must train men for it. The Negro race, like all other races, is going to be saved by its exceptional men.

The Disfranchisement of the Negro

by CHARLES W. CHESNUTT

In this paper the author presents a straightforward statement of facts concerning the disfranchisement of the Negro in the Southern States. Mr. Chesnutt, who is too well known as a writer to need any introduction to an American audience, puts the case for the Negro to the American people very plainly, and spares neither the North nor the South.

The right of American citizens of African descent, commonly called Negroes, to vote upon the same terms as other citizens of the United States, is plainly declared and firmly fixed by the Constitution. No such person is called upon to present reasons why he should possess this right: that question is foreclosed by the Constitution. The object of the elective franchise is to give representation. So long as the Constitution retains its present form, any State Constitution, or statute, which seeks, by juggling the ballot, to deny the colored race fair representation, is a clear violation of the fundamental law of the land, and a corresponding injustice to those thus deprived of this right.

For thirty-five years this has been the law. As long as it was measurably respected, the colored people made rapid strides in education, wealth, character and self-respect. This the census proves, all statements to the contrary notwithstanding. A generation has grown to manhood and womanhood under the great, inspiring freedom conferred by the Constitution and protected by the right of suffrage--protected in large degree by the mere naked right, even when its exercise was hindered or denied by unlawful means. They have developed, in every Southern community, good citizens, who, if sustained and encouraged by just laws and liberal institutions, would greatly augment their number with the passing years, and soon wipe out the reproach of ignorance, unthrift, low morals and social inefficiency, thrown at them indiscriminately and therefore unjustly, and made the excuse for the equally undiscriminating contempt of their persons and their rights. They have reduced their illiteracy nearly 50 per cent. Excluded from the institutions of higher learning in their own States, their young men hold their own, and occasionally carry away honors, in the universities of the North. They have accumulated three hundred million dollars worth of real and personal property. Individuals among them have acquired substantial wealth, and several have attained to something like national distinction in art, letters and educational leadership. They are numerously represented in the learned professions. Heavily handicapped, they have made such rapid progress that the suspicion is justified that their advancement, rather than any stagnation or retrogression, is the true secret of the virulent Southern hostility to their rights, which has so influenced Northern opinion that it stands mute, and leaves the colored people, upon whom the North conferred liberty, to the tender mercies of those who have always denied their fitness for it.

It may be said, in passing, that the word "Negro," where used in this paper, is used solely for convenience. By the census of 1890 there were 1,000,000 colored people in the country who were half, or more than half, white, and logically there must be, as in fact there are, so many who share the white blood in some degree, as to justify the assertion that the race problem in the United States concerns the welfare and the status of a mixed race. Their rights are not one whit the more sacred because of this fact; but in an argument where injustice is sought to be excused because of fundamental differences of race, it is well enough to bear in mind that the race whose rights and liberties are endangered all over this country by disfranchisement at the South, are the colored people who live in the United States to-day, and not the low-browed, man-eating savage whom the Southern white likes to set upon a block and contrast with Shakespeare and Newton and Washington and Lincoln.

Despite and in defiance of the Federal Constitution, to-day in the six Southern States of Mississippi, Louisiana, Alabama, North Carolina, South Carolina and Virginia, containing an aggregate colored population of about 6,000,000, these have been, to all intents and purposes, denied, so far as the States can effect it, the right to vote. This disfranchisement is accomplished by various methods, devised with much transparent ingenuity, the effort being in each instance to violate the spirit of the Federal Constitution by disfranchising the Negro, while seeming to respect its letter by avoiding the mention of race or color.

These restrictions fall into three groups. The first comprises a property qualification--the ownership of $300 worth or more of real or personal property (Alabama, Louisiana, Virginia and South Carolina); the payment of a poll tax (Mississippi, North Carolina, Virginia); an educational qualification--the ability to read and write (Alabama, Louisiana, North Carolina). Thus far, those who believe in a restricted suffrage everywhere, could perhaps find no reasonable fault with any one of these qualifications, applied either separately or together.

But the Negro has made such progress that these restrictions alone would perhaps not deprive him of effective representation. Hence the second group. This comprises an "understanding" clause-- the applicant must be able "to read, or understand when read to him, any clause in the Constitution" (Mississippi), or to read and explain, or to understand and explain when read to him, any section of the Constitution (Virginia); an employment qualification--the voter must be regularly employed in some lawful occupation (Alabama); a character qualification--the voter must be a person of good character and who "understands the duties and obligations of citizens under a republican (!) form of government" (Alabama).

The qualifications under the first group it will be seen, are capable of exact demonstration; those under the second group are left to the discretion and judgment of the registering officer--for in most instances these are all requirements for registration, which must precede voting.

But the first group, by its own force, and the second group, under imaginable conditions, might exclude not only the Negro vote, but a large part of the white vote. Hence, the third group, which comprises: a military service qualification--any man who went to war, willingly or unwillingly, in a good cause or a bad, is entitled to register (Ala., Va.); a prescriptive qualification, under which are included all male persons who were entitled to vote on January 1, 1867, at which date the Negro had not yet been given the right to vote; a hereditary qualification, (the so-called "grandfather" clause), whereby any son (Va.), or descendant (Ala.), of a soldier, and (N.C.) the descendant of any person who had the right to vote on January 1, 1867, inherits that right. If the voter wish to take advantage of these last provisions, which are in the nature of exceptions to a general rule, he must register within a stated time, whereupon he becomes a member of a privileged class of permanently enrolled voters not subject to any of the other restrictions.

It will be seen that these restrictions are variously combined in the different States, and it is apparent that if combined to their declared end, practically every Negro may, under color of law, be denied the right to vote, and practically every white man accorded that right. The effectiveness of these provisions to exclude the Negro vote is proved by the Alabama registration under the new State Constitution. Out of a total, by the census of 1900, of 181,471 Negro "males of voting age," less than 3,000 are registered; in Montgomery county alone, the seat of the State capital, where there are 7,000 Negro males of voting age, only 47 have been allowed to register, while in several counties not one single Negro is permitted to exercise the franchise.

These methods of disfranchisement have stood such tests as the United States Courts, including the Supreme Court, have thus far seen fit to apply, in such cases as have been before them for adjudication. These include a case based upon the "understanding" clause of the Mississippi Constitution, in which the Supreme Court held, in effect, that since there was no ambiguity in the language employed and the Negro was not directly named, the Court would not go behind the wording of the Constitution to find a meaning which discriminated against the colored voter; and the recent case of Jackson vs. Giles, brought by a colored citizen of Montgomery, Alabama, in which the Supreme Court confesses itself impotent to provide a remedy for what, by inference, it acknowledges may be a "great political wrong," carefully avoiding, however, to state that it is a wrong, although the vital prayer of the petition was for a decision upon this very point.

Now, what is the effect of this wholesale disfranchisement of colored men, upon their citizenship. The value of food to the human organism is not measured by the pains of an occasional surfeit, but by the effect of its entire deprivation. Whether a class of citizens should vote, even if not always wisely--what class does?--may best be determined by considering their condition when they are without the right to vote.

The colored people are left, in the States where they have been disfranchised, absolutely without representation, direct or indirect, in any law-making body, in any court of justice, in any branch of government--for the feeble remnant of voters left by law is so inconsiderable as to be without a shadow of power. Constituting one-eighth of the population of the whole country, two-fifths of the whole Southern people, and a majority in several States, they are not able, because disfranchised where most numerous, to send one representative to the Congress, which, by the decision in the Alabama case, is held by the Supreme Court to be the only body, outside of the State itself, competent to give relief from a great political wrong. By former decisions of the same tribunal, even Congress is impotent to protect their civil rights, the Fourteenth Amendment having long since, by the consent of the same Court, been in many respects as completely nullified as the Fifteenth Amendment is now sought to be. They have no direct representation in any Southern legislature, and no voice in determining the choice of white men who might be friendly to their rights. Nor are they able to influence the election of judges or other public officials, to whom are entrusted the protection of their lives, their liberties and their property. No judge is rendered careful, no sheriff diligent, for fear that he may offend a black constituency; the contrary is most lamentably true; day after day the catalogue of lynchings and anti-Negro riots upon every imaginable pretext, grows longer and more appalling. The country stands face to face with the revival of slavery; at the moment of this writing a federal grand jury in Alabama is uncovering a system of peonage established under cover of law.

Under the Southern program it is sought to exclude colored men from every grade of the public service; not only from the higher administrative functions, to which few of them would in any event, for a long time aspire, but from the lowest as well. A Negro may not be a constable or a policeman. He is subjected by law to many degrading discriminations. He is required to be separated from white people on railroads and street cars, and, by custom, debarred from inns and places of public entertainment. His equal right to a free public education is constantly threatened and is nowhere equitably recognized. In Georgia, as has been shown by Dr. DuBois, where the law provides for a pro rata distribution of the public school fund between the races, and where the colored school population is 48 per cent. of the total, the amount of the fund devoted to their schools is only 20 per cent. In New Orleans, with an immense colored population, many of whom are persons of means and culture, all colored public schools above the fifth grade have been abolished.

The Negro is subjected to taxation without representation, which the forefathers of this Republic made the basis of a bloody revolution.

Flushed with their local success, and encouraged by the timidity of the Courts and the indifference of public opinion, the Southern whites have carried their campaign into the national government, with an ominous degree of success. If they shall have their way, no Negro can fill any federal office, or occupy, in the public service, any position that is not menial. This is not an inference, but the openly, passionately avowed sentiment of the white South. The right to employment in the public service is an exceedingly valuable one, for which white men have struggled and fought. A vast army of men are employed in the administration of public affairs. Many avenues of employment are closed to colored men by popular prejudice. If their right to public employment is recognized, and the way to it open through the civil service, or the appointing power, or the suffrages of the people, it will prove, as it has already, a strong incentive to effort and a powerful lever for advancement. Its value to the Negro, like that of the right to vote, may be judged by the eagerness of the whites to deprive him of it.

Not only is the Negro taxed without representation in the States referred to, but he pays, through the tariff and internal revenue, a tax to a National government whose supreme judicial tribunal declares that it cannot, through the executive arm, enforce its own decrees, and, therefore, refuses to pass upon a question, squarely before it, involving a basic right of citizenship. For the decision of the Supreme Court in the Giles case, if it foreshadows the attitude which the Court will take upon other cases to the same general end which will soon come before it, is scarcely less than a reaffirmation of the Dred Scott decision; it certainly amounts to this--that in spite of the Fifteenth Amendment, colored men in the United States have no political rights which the States are bound to respect. To say this much is to say that all the privileges and immunities which Negroes henceforth enjoy, must be by favor of the whites; they are not rights. The whites have so declared; they proclaim that the country is theirs, that the Negro should be thankful that he has so much, when so much more might be withheld from him. He stands upon a lower footing than any alien; he has no government to which he may look for protection.

Moreover, the white South sends to Congress, on a basis including the Negro population, a delegation nearly twice as large as it is justly entitled to, and one which may always safely be relied upon to oppose in Congress every measure which seeks to protect the equality, or to enlarge the rights of colored citizens. The grossness of this injustice is all the more apparent since the Supreme Court, in the Alabama case referred to, has declared the legislative and political department of the government to be the only power which can right a political wrong. Under this decision still further attacks upon the liberties of the citizen may be confidently expected. Armed with the Negro's sole weapon of defense, the white South stands ready to smite down his rights. The ballot was first given to the Negro to defend him against this very thing. He needs it now far more than then, and for even stronger reasons. The 9,000,000 free colored people of to-day have vastly more to defend than the 3,000,000 hapless blacks who had just emerged from slavery. If there be those who maintain that it was a mistake to give the Negro the ballot at the time and in the manner in which it was given, let them take to heart this reflection: that to deprive him of it to-day, or to so restrict it as to leave him utterly defenseless against the present relentless attitude of the South toward his rights, will prove to be a mistake so much greater than the first, as to be no less than a crime, from which not alone the Southern Negro must suffer, but for which the nation will as surely pay the penalty as it paid for the crime of slavery. Contempt for law is death to a republic, and this one has developed alarming symptoms of the disease.

And now, having thus robbed the Negro of every political and civil right, the white South, in palliation of its course, makes a great show of magnanimity in leaving him, as the sole remnant of what he acquired through the Civil War, a very inadequate public school education, which, by the present program, is to be directed mainly towards making him a better agricultural laborer. Even this is put forward as a favor, although the Negro's property is taxed to pay for it, and his labor as well. For it is a well settled principle of political economy, that land and machinery of themselves produce nothing, and that labor indirectly pays its fair proportion of the tax upon the public's wealth. The white South seems to stand to the Negro at present as one, who, having been reluctantly compelled to release another from bondage, sees him stumbling forward and upward, neglected by his friends and scarcely yet conscious of his own strength; seizes him, binds him, and having bereft him of speech, of sight and of manhood, "yokes him with the mule" and exclaims, with a show of virtue which ought to deceive no one: "Behold how good a friend I am of yours! Have I not left you a stomach and a pair of arms, and will I not generously permit you to work for me with the one, that you may thereby gain enough to fill the other? A brain you do not need. We will relieve you of any responsibility that might seem to demand such an organ."

The argument of peace-loving Northern white men and Negro opportunists that the political power of the Negro having long ago been suppressed by unlawful means, his right to vote is a mere paper right, of no real value, and therefore to be lightly yielded for the sake of a hypothetical harmony, is fatally short-sighted. It is precisely the attitude and essentially the argument which would have surrendered to the South in the sixties, and would have left this country to rot in slavery for another generation. White men do not thus argue concerning their own rights. They know too well the value of ideals. Southern white men see too clearly the latent power of these unexercised rights. If the political power of the Negro was a nullity because of his ignorance and lack of leadership, why were they not content to leave it so, with the pleasing assurance that if it ever became effective, it would be because the Negroes had grown fit for its exercise? On the contrary, they have not rested until the possibility of its revival was apparently headed off by new State Constitutions. Nor are they satisfied with this. There is no doubt that an effort will be made to secure the repeal of the Fifteenth Amendment, and thus forestall the development of the wealthy and educated Negro, whom the South seems to anticipate as a greater menace than the ignorant ex-slave. However improbable this repeal may seem, it is not a subject to be lightly dismissed; for it is within the power of the white people of the nation to do whatever they wish in the premises--they did it once; they can do it again. The Negro and his friends should see to it that the white majority shall never wish to do anything to his hurt. There still stands, before the Negro-hating whites of the South, the specter of a Supreme Court which will interpret the Constitution to mean what it says, and what those who enacted it meant, and what the nation, which ratified it, understood, and which will find power, in a nation which goes beyond seas to administer the affairs of distant peoples, to enforce its own fundamental laws; the specter, too, of an aroused public opinion which will compel Congress and the Courts to preserve the liberties of the Republic, which are the liberties of the people. To wilfully neglect the suffrage, to hold it lightly, is to tamper with a sacred right; to yield it for anything else whatever is simply suicidal. Dropping the element of race, disfranchisement is no more than to say to the poor and poorly taught, that they must relinquish the right to defend themselves against oppression until they shall have become rich and learned, in competition with those already thus favored and possessing the ballot in addition. This is not the philosophy of history. The growth of liberty has been the constant struggle of the poor against the privileged classes; and the goal of that struggle has ever been the equality of all men before the law. The Negro who would yield this right, deserves to be a slave; he has the servile spirit. The rich and the educated can, by virtue of their influence, command many votes; can find other means of protection; the poor man has but one, he should guard it as a sacred treasure. Long ago, by fair treatment, the white leaders of the South might have bound the Negro to themselves with hoops of steel. They have not chosen to take this course, but by assuming from the beginning an attitude hostile to his rights, have never gained his confidence, and now seek by foul means to destroy where they have never sought by fair means to control.

  I have spoken of the effect of disfranchisement upon the colored race; it is to the race as a whole, that the argument of the problem is generally directed. But the unit of society in a republic is the individual, and not the race, the failure to recognize this fact being the fundamental error which has beclouded the whole discussion. The effect of disfranchisement upon the individual is scarcely less disastrous. I do not speak of the moral effect of injustice upon those who suffer from it; I refer rather to the practical consequences which may be appreciated by any mind. No country is free in which the way upward is not open for every man to try, and for every properly qualified man to attain whatever of good the community life may offer. Such a condition does not exist, at the South, even in theory, for any man of color. In no career can such a man compete with white men upon equal terms. He must not only meet the prejudice of the individual, not only the united prejudice of the white community; but lest some one should wish to treat him fairly, he is met at every turn with some legal prohibition which says, "Thou shalt not," or "Thus far shalt thou go and no farther." But the Negro race is viable; it adapts itself readily to circumstances; and being thus adaptable, there is always the temptation to

"Crook the pregnant hinges of the knee,
Where thrift may follow fawning."

He who can most skilfully balance himself upon the advancing or receding wave of white opinion concerning his race, is surest of such measure of prosperity as is permitted to men of dark skins. There are Negro teachers in the South--the privilege of teaching in their own schools is the one respectable branch of the public service still left open to them--who, for a grudging appropriation from a Southern legislature, will decry their own race, approve their own degradation, and laud their oppressors. Deprived of the right to vote, and, therefore, of any power to demand what is their due, they feel impelled to buy the tolerance of the whites at any sacrifice. If to live is the first duty of man, as perhaps it is the first instinct, then those who thus stoop to conquer may be right. But is it needful to stoop so low, and if so, where lies the ultimate responsibility for this abasement?

I shall say nothing about the moral effect of disfranchisement upon the white people, or upon the State itself. What slavery made of the Southern whites is a matter of history. The abolition of slavery gave the South an opportunity to emerge from barbarism. Present conditions indicate that the spirit which dominated slavery still curses the fair section over which that institution spread its blight.

And now, is the situation remediless? If not so, where lies the remedy? First let us take up those remedies suggested by the men who approve of disfranchisement, though they may sometimes deplore the method, or regret the necessity.

Time, we are told, heals all diseases, rights all wrongs, and is the only cure for this one. It is a cowardly argument. These people are entitled to their rights to-day, while they are yet alive to enjoy them;

and it is poor statesmanship and worse morals to nurse a present evil and thrust it forward upon a future generation for correction. The nation can no more honestly do this than it could thrust back upon a past generation the responsibility for slavery. It had to meet that responsibility; it ought to meet this one.

Education has been put forward as the great corrective--preferably industrial education. The intellect of the whites is to be educated to the point where they will so appreciate the blessings of liberty and equality, as of their own motion to enlarge and defend the Negro's rights. The Negroes, on the other hand, are to be so trained as to make them, not equal with the whites in any way--God save the mark! this would be unthinkable!--but so useful to the community that the whites will protect them rather than to lose their valuable services. Some few enthusiasts go so far as to maintain that by virtue of education the Negro will, in time, become strong enough to protect himself against any aggression of the whites; this, it may be said, is a strictly Northern view.

It is not quite clearly apparent how education alone, in the ordinary meaning of the word, is to solve, in any appreciable time, the problem of the relations of Southern white and black people. The need of education of all kinds for both races is wofully apparent. But men and nations have been free without being learned, and there have been educated slaves. Liberty has been known to languish where culture had reached a very high development. Nations do not first become rich and learned and then free, but the lesson of history has been that they first become free and then rich and learned, and oftentimes fall back into slavery again because of too great wealth, and the resulting luxury and carelessness of civic virtues. The process of education has been going on rapidly in the Southern States since the Civil War, and yet, if we take superficial indications, the rights of the Negroes are at a lower ebb than at any time during the thirty-five years of their freedom, and the race prejudice more intense and uncompromising. It is not apparent that educated Southerners are less rancorous than others in their speech concerning the Negro, or less hostile in their attitude toward his rights. It is their voice alone that we have heard in this discussion; and if, as they state, they are liberal in their views as compared with the more ignorant whites, then God save the Negro!

I was told, in so many words, two years ago, by the Superintendent of Public Schools of a Southern city that "there was no place in the modern world for the Negro, except under the ground." If gentlemen holding such opinions are to instruct the white youth of the South, would it be at all surprising if these, later on, should devote a portion of their leisure to the improvement of civilization by putting under the ground as many of this superfluous race as possible?

The sole excuse made in the South for the prevalent injustice to the Negro is the difference in race, and the inequalities and antipathies resulting therefrom. It has nowhere been declared as a part of the Southern program that the Negro, when educated, is to be given a fair representation in government or an equal opportunity in life; the contrary has been strenuously asserted; education can never make of him anything but a Negro, and, therefore, essentially inferior, and not to be safely trusted with any degree of power. A system of education which would tend to soften the asperities and lessen the inequalities between the races would be of inestimable value. An education which by a rigid separation of the races from the kindergarten to the university, fosters this racial antipathy, and is directed toward emphasizing the superiority of one class and the inferiority of another, might easily have disastrous, rather than beneficial results. It would render the oppressing class more powerful to injure, the oppressed quicker to perceive and keener to resent the injury, without proportionate power of defense. The same assimilative education which is given at the North to all children alike, whereby native and foreign, black and white, are taught side by side in every grade of instruction, and are compelled by the exigencies of discipline to keep their prejudices in abeyance, and are given the opportunity to learn and appreciate one another's good qualities, and to establish friendly relations which may exist throughout life, is absent from the Southern system of education, both of the past and as proposed for the future. Education is in a broad sense a remedy for all social ills; but the disease we have to deal with now is not only constitutional but acute. A wise physician does not simply give a tonic for a diseased limb, or a high fever; the patient might be dead before the constitutional remedy could become effective. The evils of slavery, its injury to whites and blacks, and to the body politic, was clearly perceived and acknowledged by the educated leaders of the South as far back as the Revolutionary War and the Constitutional Convention, and yet they made no effort to abolish it. Their remedy was the same--time, education, social and economic development;--and yet a bloody war was necessary to destroy slavery and put its spirit temporarily to sleep. When the South and its friends are ready to propose a system of education which will recognize and teach the equality of all men before the law, the potency of education alone to settle the race problem will be more clearly apparent.

At present even good Northern men, who wish to educate the Negroes, feel impelled to buy this privilege from the none too eager white South, by conceding away the civil and political rights of those whom they would benefit. They have, indeed, gone farther than the Southerners themselves in approving the disfranchisement of the colored race. Most Southern men, now that they have carried their point and disfranchised the Negro, are willing to admit, in the language of a recent number of the Charleston Evening Post , that "the attitude of the Southern white man toward the Negro is incompatible with the fundamental ideas of the republic." It remained for our Clevelands and Abbotts and Parkhursts to assure them that their unlawful course was right and justifiable, and for the most distinguished Negro leader to declare that "every revised Constitution throughout the Southern States has put a premium upon intelligence, ownership of property, thrift and character." So does every penitentiary sentence put a premium upon good conduct; but it is poor consolation to the one unjustly condemned, to be told that he may shorten his sentence somewhat by good behavior. Dr. Booker T. Washington, whose language is quoted above, has, by his eminent services in the cause of education, won deserved renown. If he has seemed, at times, to those jealous of the best things for their race, to decry the higher education, it can easily be borne in mind that his career is bound up in the success of an industrial school; hence any undue stress which he may put upon that branch of education may safely be ascribed to the natural zeal of the promoter, without detracting in any degree from the essential value of his teachings in favor of manual training, thrift and character-building. But Mr. Washington's prominence as an educational leader, among a race whose prominent leaders are so few, has at times forced him, perhaps reluctantly, to express himself in regard to the political condition of his people, and here his utterances have not always been so wise nor so happy. He has declared himself in favor of a restricted suffrage, which at present means, for his own people, nothing less than complete loss of representation--indeed it is only in that connection that the question has been seriously mooted; and he has advised them to go slow in seeking to enforce their civil and political rights, which, in effect, means silent submission to injustice. Southern white men may applaud this advice as wise, because it fits in with their purposes; but Senator McEnery of Louisiana, in a recent article in the Independent , voices the Southern white opinion of such acquiescence when he says: "What other race would have submitted so many years to slavery without complaint? What other race would have submitted so quietly to disfranchisement? These facts stamp his (the Negro's) inferiority to the white race." The time to philosophize about the good there is in evil, is not while its correction is still possible, but, if at all, after all hope of correction is past. Until then it calls for nothing but rigorous condemnation. To try to read any good thing into these fraudulent Southern constitutions, or to accept them as an accomplished fact, is to condone a crime against one's race. Those who commit crime should bear the odium. It is not a pleasing spectacle to see the robbed applaud the robber. Silence were better.

It has become fashionable to question the wisdom of the Fifteenth Amendment. I believe it to have been an act of the highest statesmanship, based upon the fundamental idea of this Republic, entirely justified by conditions; experimental in its nature, perhaps, as every new thing must be, but just in principle; a choice between methods, of which it seemed to the great statesmen of that epoch the wisest and the best, and essentially the most just, bearing in mind the interests of the freedmen and the Nation, as well as the feelings of the Southern whites; never fairly tried, and therefore, not yet to be justly condemned. Not one of those who condemn it, has been able, even in the light of subsequent events, to suggest a better method by which the liberty and civil rights of the freedmen and their descendants could have been protected. Its abandonment, as I have shown, leaves this liberty and these rights frankly without any guaranteed protection. All the education which philanthropy or the State could offer as a substitute for equality of rights, would be a poor exchange; there is no defensible reason why they should not go hand in hand, each encouraging and strengthening the other. The education which one can demand as a right is likely to do more good than the education for which one must sue as a favor.

The chief argument against Negro suffrage, the insistently proclaimed argument, worn threadbare in Congress, on the platform, in the pulpit, in the press, in poetry, in fiction, in impassioned rhetoric, is the reconstruction period. And yet the evils of that period were due far more to the venality and indifference of white men than to the incapacity of black voters. The revised Southern Constitutions adopted under reconstruction reveal a higher statesmanship than any which preceded or have followed them, and prove that the freed voters could as easily have been led into the paths of civic righteousness as into those of misgovernment. Certain it is that under reconstruction the civil and political rights of all men were more secure in those States than they have ever been since. We will hear less of the evils of reconstruction, now that the bugaboo has served its purpose by disfranchising the Negro, it will be laid aside for a time while the nation discusses the political corruption of great cities; the scandalous conditions in Rhode Island; the evils attending reconstruction in the Philippines, and the scandals in the postoffice department--for none of which, by the way, is the Negro charged with any responsibility, and for none of which is the restriction of the suffrage a remedy seriously proposed. Rhode Island is indeed the only Northern State which has a property qualification for the franchise!

There are three tribunals to which the colored people may justly appeal for the protection of their rights: the United States Courts, Congress and public opinion. At present all three seem mainly indifferent to any question of human rights under the Constitution. Indeed, Congress and the Courts merely follow public opinion, seldom lead it. Congress never enacts a measure which is believed to oppose public opinion;--your Congressman keeps his ear to the ground. The high, serene atmosphere of the Courts is not impervious to its voice; they rarely enforce a law contrary to public opinion, even the Supreme Court being able, as Charles Sumner once put it, to find a reason for every decision it may wish to render; or, as experience has shown, a method to evade any question which it cannot decently decide in accordance with public opinion. The art of straddling is not confined to the political arena. The Southern situation has been well described by a colored editor in Richmond: "When we seek relief at the hands of Congress, we are informed that our plea involves a legal question, and we are referred to the Courts. When we appeal to the Courts, we are gravely told that the question is a political one, and that we must go to Congress. When Congress enacts remedial legislation, our enemies take it to the Supreme Court, which promptly declares it unconstitutional." The Negro might chase his rights round and round this circle until the end of time, without finding any relief.

Yet the Constitution is clear and unequivocal in its terms, and no Supreme Court can indefinitely continue to construe it as meaning anything but what it says. This Court should be bombarded with suits until it makes some definite pronouncement, one way or the other, on the broad question of the constitutionality of the disfranchising Constitutions of the Southern States. The Negro and his friends will then have a clean-cut issue to take to the forum of public opinion, and a distinct ground upon which to demand legislation for the enforcement of the Federal Constitution. The case from Alabama was carried to the Supreme Court expressly to determine the constitutionality of the Alabama Constitution. The Court declared itself without jurisdiction, and in the same breath went into the merits of the case far enough to deny relief, without passing upon the real issue. Had it said, as it might with absolute justice and perfect propriety, that the Alabama Constitution is a bold and impudent violation of the Fifteenth Amendment, the purpose of the lawsuit would have been accomplished and a righteous cause vastly strengthened.

But public opinion cannot remain permanently indifferent to so vital a question. The agitation is already on. It is at present largely academic, but is slowly and resistlessly, forcing itself into politics, which is the medium through which republics settle such questions. It cannot much longer be contemptuously or indifferently elbowed aside. The South itself seems bent upon forcing the question to an issue, as, by its arrogant assumptions, it brought on the Civil War. From that section, too, there come now and then, side by side with tales of Southern outrage, excusing voices, which at the same time are accusing voices; which admit that the white South is dealing with the Negro unjustly and unwisely; that the Golden Rule has been forgotten; that the interests of white men alone have been taken into account, and that their true interests as well are being sacrificed. There is a silent white South, uneasy in conscience, darkened in counsel, groping for the light, and willing to do the right. They are as yet a feeble folk, their voices scarcely audible above the clamor of the mob. May their convictions ripen into wisdom, and may their numbers and their courage increase! If the class of Southern white men of whom Judge Jones of Alabama, is so noble a representative, are supported and encouraged by a righteous public opinion at the North, they may, in time, become the dominant white South, and we may then look for wisdom and justice in the place where, so far as the Negro is concerned, they now seem well-nigh strangers. But even these gentlemen will do well to bear in mind that so long as they discriminate in any way against the Negro's equality of right, so long do they set class against class and open the door to every sort of discrimination. There can be no middle ground between justice and injustice, between the citizen and the serf.

It is not likely that the North, upon the sober second thought, will permit the dearly-bought results of the Civil War to be nullified by any change in the Constitution. As long as the Fifteenth Amendment stands, the rights of colored citizens are ultimately secure. There were would-be despots in England after the granting of Magna Charta; but it outlived them all, and the liberties of the English people are secure. There was slavery in this land after the Declaration of Independence, yet the faces of those who love liberty have ever turned to that immortal document. So will the Constitution and its principles outlive the prejudices which would seek to overthrow it.

What colored men of the South can do to secure their citizenship to-day, or in the immediate future, is not very clear. Their utterances on political questions, unless they be to concede away the political rights of their race, or to soothe the consciences of white men by suggesting that the problem is insoluble except by some slow remedial process which will become effectual only in the distant future, are received with scant respect--could scarcely, indeed, be otherwise received, without a voting constituency to back them up,-- and must be cautiously made, lest they meet an actively hostile reception. But there are many colored men at the North, where their civil and political rights in the main are respected. There every honest man has a vote, which he may freely cast, and which is reasonably sure to be fairly counted. When this race develops a sufficient power of combination, under adequate leadership,--and there are signs already that this time is near at hand,--the Northern vote can be wielded irresistibly for the defense of the rights of their Southern brethren.

In the meantime the Northern colored men have the right of free speech, and they should never cease to demand their rights, to clamor for them, to guard them jealously, and insistently to invoke law and public sentiment to maintain them. He who would be free must learn to protect his freedom. Eternal vigilance is the price of liberty. He who would be respected must respect himself. The best friend of the Negro is he who would rather see, within the borders of this republic one million free citizens of that race, equal before the law, than ten million cringing serfs existing by a contemptuous sufferance. A race that is willing to survive upon any other terms is scarcely worthy of consideration.

The direct remedy for the disfranchisement of the Negro lies through political action. One scarcely sees the philosophy of distinguishing between a civil and a political right. But the Supreme Court has recognized this distinction and has designated Congress as the power to right a political wrong. The Fifteenth Amendment gives Congress power to enforce its provisions. The power would seem to be inherent in government itself; but anticipating that the enforcement of the Amendment might involve difficulty, they made the superorogatory declaration. Moreover, they went further, and passed laws by which they provided for such enforcement. These the Supreme Court has so far declared insufficient. It is for Congress to make more laws. It is for colored men and for white men who are not content to see the blood-bought results of the Civil War nullified, to urge and direct public opinion to the point where it will demand stringent legislation to enforce the Fourteenth and Fifteenth Amendments. This demand will rest in law, in morals and in true statesmanship; no difficulties attending it could be worse than the present ignoble attitude of the Nation toward its own laws and its own ideals--without courage to enforce them, without conscience to change them, the United States presents the spectacle of a Nation drifting aimlessly, so far as this vital, National problem is concerned, upon the sea of irresolution, toward the maelstrom of anarchy.

The right of Congress, under the Fourteenth Amendment, to reduce Southern representation can hardly be disputed. But Congress has a simpler and more direct method to accomplish the same end. It is the sole judge of the qualifications of its own members, and the sole judge of whether any member presenting his credentials has met those qualifications. It can refuse to seat any member who comes from a district where voters have been disfranchised: it can judge for itself whether this has been done, and there is no appeal from its decision.

If, when it has passed a law, any Court shall refuse to obey its behests, it can impeach the judges. If any president refuse to lend the executive arm of the government to the enforcement of the law, it can impeach the president. No such extreme measures are likely to be necessary for the enforcement of the Fourteenth and Fifteenth Amendments--and the Thirteenth, which is also threatened--but they are mentioned as showing that Congress is supreme; and Congress proceeds, the House directly, the Senate indirectly, from the people and is governed by public opinion. If the reduction of Southern representation were to be regarded in the light of a bargain by which the Fifteenth Amendment was surrendered, then it might prove fatal to liberty. If it be inflicted as a punishment and a warning, to be followed by more drastic measures if not sufficient, it would serve a useful purpose. The Fifteenth Amendment declares that the right to vote shall not be denied or abridged on account of color; and any measure adopted by Congress should look to that end. Only as the power to injure the Negro in Congress is reduced thereby, would a reduction of representation protect the Negro; without other measures it would still leave him in the hands of the Southern whites, who could safely be trusted to make him pay for their humiliation.

Finally, there is, somewhere in the Universe a "Power that works for righteousness," and that leads men to do justice to one another. To this power, working upon the hearts and consciences of men, the Negro can always appeal. He has the right upon his side, and in the end the right will prevail. The Negro will, in time, attain to full manhood and citizenship throughout the United States. No better guaranty of this is needed than a comparison of his present with his past. Toward this he must do his part, as lies within his power and his opportunity. But it will be, after all, largely a white man's conflict, fought out in the forum of the public conscience. The Negro, though eager enough when opportunity offered, had comparatively little to do with the abolition of slavery, which was a vastly more formidable task than will be the enforcement of the Fifteenth Amendment.

The Negro and the Law

by WILFORD H. SMITH

The law and how it is dodged by enactments infringing upon the rights guaranteed to the freedmen by constitutional amendment. A powerful plea for justice for the Negro.

The colored people in the United States are indebted to the beneficent provisions of the 13th, 14th and 15th amendments to the Constitution of the United States, for the establishment of their freedom and citizenship, and it is to these mainly they must look for the maintenance of their liberty and the protection of their civil rights. These amendments followed close upon the Emancipation Proclamation issued January 1st, 1863, by President Lincoln, and his call for volunteers, which was answered by more than three hundred thousand negro soldiers, who, during three years of military service, helped the Union arms to victory at Appomattox. Standing in the shadow of the awful calamity and deep distress of the civil war, and grateful to God for peace and victory over the rebellion, the American people, who upheld the Union, rose to the sublime heights of doing justice to the former slaves, who had grown and multiplied with the country from the early settlement at Jamestown. It looked like an effort to pay them back for their years of faithfulness and unrequited toil, by not only making them free but placing them on equal footing with themselves in the fundamental law. Certainly, they intended at least, that they should have as many rights under the Constitution as are given to white naturalized citizens who come to this country from all the nations of Europe.

The 13th amendment provides that neither slavery nor involuntary servitude, except as a punishment for crime, whereof the party shall have been duly convicted, shall exist in the United States or any place subject to their jurisdiction.

The 14th amendment provides in section one, that all persons born or naturalized in the United States and subject to the jurisdiction thereof, are citizens of the United States, and of the State wherein they reside. No State shall make or enforce any law which shall abridge the privileges or immunities of citizens of the United States, nor shall any State deprive any person of life, liberty or property without due process of law, nor deny to any person within its jurisdiction the equal protection of the law.

The 15th amendment provides that the right of citizens of the United States to vote shall not be denied or abridged by the United States, or by any State on account of race, color, or previous condition of servitude.

Chief Justice Waite, in the case of the United States vs. Cruikshank, 92nd U.S. 542, said:--

"The 14th amendment prohibits a State from denying to any person within its jurisdiction the equal protection of the law. The equality of the rights of citizens is a principle of republicanism. Every Republican government is in duty bound to protect all its citizens in the enjoyment of this principle if within its power."

The same Chief Justice, in the case of the United States vs. Reese, 92nd U.S. 214, said:

"The 15th amendment does not confer the right of suffrage upon anyone. It prevents the States or the United States from giving preference in this particular to one citizen of the United States over another, on account of race, color or previous condition of servitude. Before its adoption this could be done. It was as much within the power of a State to exclude citizens of the United States from voting on account of race and color, as it was on account of age, property or education. Now it is not."

Notwithstanding the manifest meaning of equality of citizenship contained in the constitutional amendments, it was found necessary to reinforce them by a civil rights law, enacted by the Congress of the United States, March 1st, 1875, entitled, "An Act To Protect All Citizens In Their Civil and Legal Rights." Its preamble and first section are as follows:--Preamble: "Whereas, it is essential to just government we recognize the equality of all men before the law, and hold that it is the duty of government in its dealings with the people to mete out equal and exact justice to all, of whatever nativity, race, color or persuasion, religious or political, and it being the appropriate object of legislation to enact great fundamental principles into law, therefore,

"Be it enacted that all persons within the jurisdiction of the United States shall be entitled to the full and equal enjoyment of the accommodations, advantages, facilities and privileges of inns, public conveyances on land or water, theatres and other places of public amusement, subject only to the conditions and limitations established by law, and applicable alike to citizens of every race and color, regardless to any previous condition of servitude."

The Supreme Court of the United States has held this salutary law unconstitutional and void as applied to the States, but binding in the District of Columbia, and the Territories over which the government of the United States has control.--Civil Rights cases 109 U.S. 63. Since the Supreme Court's ruling, many Northern and Western States have enacted similar civil rights laws. Equality of citizenship in the United States suffered a severe blow when the civil rights bill was struck down by the Supreme Court. The colored people looked upon the decision as unsound, and prompted by race prejudice. It was clear that the amendments to the Constitution were adopted to secure not only their freedom, but their equal civil rights, and by ratifying the amendments the several States conceded to the Federal government the power and authority of maintaining not alone their freedom, but their equal civil rights in the United States as well.

The Federal Supreme Court put a narrow interpretation on the Constitution, rather than a liberal one in favor of equal rights; in marked contrast to a recent decision of the Appellate Division of the Supreme Court of New York in a civil rights case arising under the statute of New York, Burks vs. Bosso, 81 N.Y. Supp, 384. The New York Supreme Court held this language: "The liberation of the slaves, and the suppression of the rebellion, was supplemented by the amendments to the national Constitution according to the colored people their civil rights and investing them with citizenship. The amendments indicated a clear purpose to secure equal rights to the black people with the white race. The legislative intent must control, and that may be gathered from circumstances inducing the act. Where that intent has been unvaryingly manifested in one direction, and that in the prohibition of any discrimination against a large class of citizens, the courts should not hesitate to keep apace with legislative purpose. We must remember that the slightest trace of African blood places a man under the ban of belonging to that race. However respectable and whatever he may be, he is ostracized socially, and when the policy of the law is against extending the prohibition of his civil rights, a liberal, rather than a narrow interpretation should be given to enactments evidencing the intent to eliminate race discrimination, as far as that can be accomplished by legislative intervention."

The statutory enactments and recent Constitutions of most of the former slave-holding States, show that they have never looked with favor upon the amendments to the national Constitution. They rather regard them as war measures designed by the North to humiliate and punish the people of those States lately in rebellion.

While in the main they accept the 13th amendment and concede that the negro should have personal freedom, they have never been altogether in harmony with the spirit and purposes of the 14th and 15th amendments. There seems to be a distinct and positive fear on the part of the South that if the negro is given a man's chance, and is accorded equal civil rights with white men on the juries, on common carriers, and in public places, that it will in some way lead to his social equality. This fallacious argument is persisted in, notwithstanding the well-known fact, that although the Jews are the leaders in the wealth and commerce of the South, their civil equality has never, except in rare instances, led to any social intermingling with the Southern whites.

Holding these views the Southern people in 1875, found means to overcome the Republican majorities in all the re-constructed States, and practically drove the negroes out of the law-making bodies of all those States. So that, now in all the Southern States, so far as can be ascertained, there is not one negro sitting as a representative in any of the law-making bodies. The next step was to deny them representation on the grand and petit juries in the State courts, through Jury Commissioners, who excluded them from the panels.

To be taxed without representation is a serious injustice in a republic whose foundations are laid upon the principle of "no taxation without representation." But serious as this phase of the case must appear, infinitely more serious is the case when we consider the fact that they are likewise excluded from the grand and petit juries in all the State courts, with the fewest and rarest exceptions. The courts sit in judgment upon their lives and liberties, and dispose of their dearest earthly possessions. They are not entitled to life, liberty or property if the courts should decide they are not, and yet in this all-important tribunal they are denied all voice, except as parties and witnesses, and here and there a negro lawyer is permitted to appear. One vote on the grand jury might prevent an indictment, and save disgrace and the risk of public trial; while one vote on the petit jury might save a life or a term of imprisonment, for an innocent person pursued and persecuted by powerful enemies.

With no voice in the making of the laws, which they are bound to obey, nor in their administration by the courts, thus tied and helpless, the negroes were proscribed by a system of legal enactments intended to wholly nullify the letter and spirit of the war amendments to the national organic law. This crusade was begun by enacting a system of Jim-Crow car laws in all the Southern States, so that now the Jim-Crow cars run from the Gulf of Mexico into the national capital. They are called, "Separate Car Laws," providing for separate but equal accommodations for whites and negroes. Though fair on their face, they are everywhere known to discriminate against the colored people in their administration, and were intended to humiliate and degrade them.

Setting apart separate places for negroes on public carriers, is just as repugnant to the spirit and intent of the national Constitution, as would be a law compelling all Jews or all Roman Catholics to occupy compartments specially set apart for them on account of their religion. If these statutes were not especially aimed at the negro, an arrangement of different fares, such as first, second and third classes, would have been far more just and preferable, and would have enabled the refined and exclusive of both races to avoid the presence of the coarse and vicious, by selecting the more expensive fare. Still these laws have been upheld by the Federal Supreme Court, and pronounced not in conflict with the amendments to the Constitution of the United States.

City ordinances providing for separate street cars for white and colored passengers, are in force in Atlanta, New Orleans, and in nearly all the cities of the South. In all the principal cities of Alabama, a certain portion of the street cars is set apart and marked for negroes. The conductors are clothed with the authority of determining to what race the passenger belongs, and may arrest persons refusing to obey his orders. It is often a very difficult task to determine to what race some passengers belong, there being so many dark-white persons that might be mistaken for negroes, and persons known as negroes who are as fair as any white person.

In the State of Georgia, a negro cannot purchase a berth in a sleeping car, under any circumstances, no matter where his destination, owing to the following statute enacted December 20th, 1899: "Sleeping car companies, and all railroads operating sleeping cars in this State, shall separate the white and colored races, and shall not permit them to occupy the same compartment; provided, that nothing in this act shall be construed to compel sleeping car companies or railroads operating sleeping cars, to carry persons of color in sleeping or parlor cars; provided also, that this act shall not apply to colored nurses or servants travelling with their employers." The violation of this statute is a misdemeanor.

Article 45, section 639 of the statutes of Georgia, 1895, makes it a misdemeanor to keep or confine white and colored convicts together, or to chain them together going to and from work. There is also a statute in Georgia requiring that a separate tax list be kept in every county, of the property of white and colored persons. Both races generally approve the laws prohibiting inter-marriages between white and colored persons, which seem to be uniform throughout the Southern States.

Florida seems to have gone a step further than the rest, and by sections 2612 and 2613, Revised Statutes, 1892, it is made a misdemeanor for a white man and a colored woman, and vice versa, to sleep under the same roof at night, occupying the same room. Florida is entitled to credit, however, for a statute making marriages between white and colored persons prior to 1866, where they continue to live together, valid and binding to all intents and purposes.

In addition to this forced separation of the races by law, "from the cradle to the grave," there is yet a sadder and more deplorable separation, in the almost universal disposition to leave the negroes wholly and severely to themselves in their home life and religious life, by the white Christian people of the South, distinctly manifesting no concern in their moral and religious development.

In Georgia and the Carolinas, and all the Gulf States (except Texas, where the farm labor is mostly white) the negroes on the farms are held by a system of laws which prevents them from leaving the plantations, and enables the landlord to punish them by fine and imprisonment for any alleged breach of contract. In the administration of these laws they are virtually made slaves to the landlord, as long as they are in debt, and it is wholly in the power of the landlord to forever keep them in debt.

By section 355, of the Criminal Code of South Carolina, 1902, it is made a misdemeanor to violate a contract to work and labor on a farm, subject to a fine of not less than five dollars, and more than one hundred dollars, or imprisonment for not less than ten days, or more than thirty. It is also made a misdemeanor to employ any farm laborer while under contract with another, or to persuade or entice a farm laborer to leave his employer.

The Georgia laws are a little stronger in this respect than the laws of the other States. By section 121, of the Code of Georgia, 1895, it is provided, "that if any person shall, by offering higher wages, or in any other way entice, persuade or decoy, or attempt to entice, persuade or decoy any farm laborer from his employer, he shall be guilty of a misdemeanor." Again, by act of December 17th, 1901, the Georgia Legislature passed a law making it an offense to rent land, or furnish land to a farm laborer, after he has contracted with another landlord, without first obtaining the consent of the first landlord.

The presence of large numbers of negroes in the towns and cities of the South and North can be accounted for by such laws as the above, administered by ignorant country magistrates, in nearly all cases the pliant tools of the landlords.

The boldest and most open violation of the negro's rights under the Federal Constitution, was the enactment of the grand-father clauses, and understanding clauses in the new Constitutions of Louisiana, Alabama, the Carolinas, and Virginia, which have had the effect to deprive the great body of them of the right to vote in those States, for no other reason than their race and color. Although thus depriving him of his vote, and all voice in the State governments at the South, in all of them his property is taxed to pay pensions to Confederate soldiers, who fought to continue him in slavery. The fact is, the franchise had been practically taken from the negroes in the South since 1876, by admitted fraudulent methods and intimidation in elections, but it was not until late years that this nullification of the amendments was enacted into State Constitutions.

This brings me to the proposition that it is mainly in the enforcement, or the administration of the laws, however fair and equal they may appear on their face, that the constitutional rights of negroes to equal protection and treatment are denied, not only in the South but in many Northern States. There are noble exceptions, however, of high-toned honorable gentlemen on the bench as trial judges, and Supreme Court justices, in the South, who without regard to consequences have stood for fairness and justice to the negro in their courts.

With the population of the South distinctly divided into two classes, not the rich and poor, not the educated and ignorant, not the moral and immoral, but simply whites and blacks, all negroes being generally regarded as inferior and not entitled to the same rights as any white person, it is bound to be a difficult matter to obtain fair and just results, when there is any sort of conflict between the races. The negro realizes this, and knows that he is at an immense disadvantage when he is forced to litigate with a white man in civil matters, and much more so when he is charged with a crime by a white person.

The juries in the South almost always reject the testimony of any number of negroes if given in opposition to that of a white witness, and this is true in many instances, no matter how unreasonable or inconsistent the testimony of the white witness may be. Jurors in the South have been heard to admit that they would be socially ostracized if they brought in a verdict upon colored testimony alone, in opposition to white testimony.

Perhaps it can be best explained how the negro fares in the courts of the South by giving a few cases showing how justice is administered to him:

A negro boy was brought to the bar for trial before a police magistrate, in a Southern capital city, charged with assault and battery on a white boy about the same age, but a little larger. The testimony showed that the white boy had beat the negro on several previous occasions as he passed on his way to school, and each time the negro showed no disposition to fight. On the morning of the charge he attacked the negro and attempted to cut him with a knife, because the negro's mother had reported to the white boy's mother the previous assaults, and asked her to chastise him. The colored boy in trying to keep from being cut was compelled to fight, and got the advantage and threw the white boy down and blacked his eyes. The magistrate on this evidence fined the negro twenty-five dollars. The mother of the negro having once been a servant for the magistrate, found courage to rise, and said: "Jedge, yo Honer, can I speak?" The magistrate replied, "Yes, go on." She said, "Well, Jedge, my boy is ben tellin' me about dis white boy meddlin' him on his way to school, but I would not let my boy fight, 'cause I 'tole him he couldn't git no jestice in law. But he had no other way to go to school 'ceptin' gwine dat way; and den jedge, dis white chile is bigger an my chile and jumped on him fust with a knife for nothin', befo' my boy tetched him. Jedge I am a po' woman, and washes fur a livin', and ain't got nobody to help me, and can't raise all dat money. I think dat white boy's mammy ought to pay half of dis fine." By this time her voice had become stifled by her tears. The judge turned to the mother of the white boy and said, "Madam, are you willing to pay half of this fine?" She answered, "Yes, Your Honor." And the judge changed the order to a fine of $12.50 each, against both boys.

A celebrated case in point reported in the books is, George Maury vs. The State of Miss., 68 Miss. 605. I reproduce the court's statement of the case:--"This is an appeal from the Circuit Court of Kemper County. Appellant was convicted of murder and sentenced to imprisonment for life. He appears in this court without counsel. The facts are briefly these: One, Nicholson, a white man, accompanied by his little son seven years old, was driving an ox team along a public road; he had occasion to stop and the oxen were driven by his son; defendant, a negro, also in an ox wagon, was going along the road in an opposite direction, and met Nicholson's wagon in charge of the little boy. It was after dark, and when the wagons met, according to the testimony of Nicholson, the defendant insultingly demanded of the boy to give the way, and cursed and abused him. Nicholson, hearing the colloquy, hurried to the scene and a fight ensued between him and Maury, in which the latter got the advantage, inflicting severe blows upon Nicholson. This occurred on Thursday, and on the following Sunday night, Nicholson, in company with eleven or twelve of his friends, rode to the farm of Maury, and after sending several of their number to ascertain if he was at home, rode rapidly into his yard and called for him. Not finding him, they proceeded to search the premises, and found several colored men shut up in the smoke house, the door of which some of the searching party had broken open. Maury, the accused, was not found there, and about that time some one called out, "Here is George." Some of the party then started in the direction of the cotton house from which the voice proceeded, when a volley was fired from it, and two of the searching party were killed, one of whom was the son of the former owner of the defendant, and the other a brother-in-law of Nicholson. The members of the raiding party testified that their purpose in going to the home of the defendant was merely to arrest him. It was, however, shown that Nicholson, immediately after the fight on Thursday, informed Cobb, and Cobb between Thursday and Sunday night collected the men who joined in the raid. No affidavit for the arrest of Maury had been made, and none of the party had any warrant, or made any announcement to the defendant or his family, of the object of their visit. The accused who testified in his own behalf, denied that he was at home at the time of the shooting, and says he fled before the raiding party arrived. He also contradicted Nicholson in his account of the difficulty with him, and denies that he spoke harshly to the child." Chief Justice Campbell, in delivering the opinion of the court said, "It is inconceivable that the crime of murder is predicable of the facts disclosed by the evidence in this case. The time and place and circumstances of the killing forbid any such conclusion as a verdict of guilty of murder." The judgment of the trial court was reversed.

This same Chief Justice, in the case of Monroe vs. Mississippi, 71 Miss. 201, where a negro was convicted of rape, makes use of the following brave and noble language, reversing the case on the ground of the insufficiency of the evidence: "We might greatly lighten our labors by deferring in all cases to the verdict approved by the presiding judge as to the facts, but our duty is to administer justice without respect of persons, and do equal right to the poor and the rich. Hence the disposition, which we are not ashamed to confess we have, to guard jealously the rights of the poor and friendless and despised, and to be astute as far as we properly may, against injustice, whether proceeding from wilfulness or indifference."

The country has produced no abler jurist, nor the South no greater man than Ex-Chief Justice Campbell of Mississippi. If the counsel of such men as he and Chief Justice Garret of the Court of Civil Appeals of Texas, could obtain in the South, there would be no problem between the races. All would be contented because justice would be administered to the whites and blacks alike.

In the administration of the suffrage sections under the new Constitutions of the South by the partisan boards of registrars, the same discrimination against negroes was practiced. Their methods are of more or less interest. The plan was to exclude all negroes from the electorate without excluding a single white man. Under the Alabama Constitution, a soldier in the Civil War, either on the Federal or Confederate side, is entitled to qualification. When a negro goes up to register as a soldier he is asked for his discharge. When he presents it he is asked, "How do we know that you are the man whose name is written in this discharge? Bring us two white men whom we know and who will swear that you have not found this paper, and that they know that you were a soldier in the company and regiment in which you claim to have been." This, of course, could not be done, and the ex-soldier who risked his life for the Union is denied the right to vote.

The same Constitution provides that if not a soldier or the legal descendant of one, an elector must be of good character and understand the duties and obligations of citizenship under a Republican form of government. When a negro claims qualifications under the good character and understanding clauses he is put through an examination similar to the following:

"What is a republican form of government?

"What is a limited monarchy?

"What islands did the United States come into possession of by the Spanish-American War?

"What is the difference between Jeffersonian Democracy and Calhoun principles, as compared to the Monroe Doctrine?

"If the Nicaragua Canal is cut, what will be the effect if the Pacific Ocean is two feet higher than the Atlantic?" Should these questions be answered satisfactorily, the negro must still produce two white men known to the registrars to testify to his good character. A remarkable exception in the treatment of negroes by the registrars of Dallas county, Alabama, is shown in the following account taken from the Montgomery Advertiser:--

"An old negro barber by the name of Edward E. Harris, stepped in before the registrars, hat in hand, humble and polite, with a kindly smile on his face. He respectfully asked to be registered. He signed the application and waited a few minutes until the registrars had disposed of some other matters, and being impressed with his respectful bearing, some member of the board commenced to ask a few questions. The old man told his story in a straight forward manner. He said: "Gentlemen, I am getting to be a pretty old man. I was born here in the South, and I followed my young master through all of the campaigns in Virginia, when Mas' Bob Lee made it so warm for the Yankees. But our luck left us at Gettysburg. The Yankees got around in our rear there, and I got a bullet in the back of my head, and one in my leg before I got out of that scrape. But I was not hurt much, and my greatest anxiety was about my young master, Mr. John Holly, who was a member of the Bur Rifles, 18th Mississippi. He was a private and enlisted at Jackson, Miss.

"He could not be found the first day; I looked all among the dead on the battle field for him and he was not there. Next day I got a permit to go through the hospitals, and I looked into the face of every soldier closely, in the hope of finding my young master. After many hours of searching I found him, but he was dangerously wounded. I stayed by his side, wounded as I was, for three long weeks, but he gradually grew worse and then he died. I went out with the body and saw it buried as decently as I could, and then I went back to Jackson and told the young mistress how brave he was in battle, how good he was to me, and told her all the words he had sent her, as he lay there on that rude cot in the hospital. That is my record as a Confederate soldier, and if you gentlemen care to give me a certificate of registration, I would be much obliged to you." It is needless to say that old Ed. Harris got his certificate.

It is insisted upon by the leaders of public opinion at the South, that negroes should not be given equal political and civil rights with white men, defined by law and enforceable by the courts; but that they should be content to strive to deserve the good wishes and friendly feeling of the whites, and if the South is let alone, they will see to it that negroes get becoming treatment.

While there is a large number of the high-toned, chivalrous element of the old master class yet living, who would stand by the negro and not permit him to be wronged if they could prevent it, yet they are powerless to control the great mass of the poor whites who are most bitter in their prejudices against the negro. They should also bear in mind that the old master class is rapidly passing way, and that there is constantly an influx of foreigners to the South, and in less than fifty years the Italians, or some other foreign nationality, may be the ruling class in all the Southern States; and the negro, deprived of all political and civil rights by the Constitution and laws, would be wholly at the mercy of a people without sympathy for him.

In order to show the fallacy and the wrong and injustice of this doctrine, and how helplessly exposed it leaves the negro to the prejudices of the poor whites, I relate a tragedy in the life of a friend of mine, who was well known and respected in the town of Rayville, Louisiana.

Sewall Smith, for many years ran the leading barber shop for whites in the town of Rayville, and was well-liked and respected by the leading white men of the entire parish. At the suggestion of his customers he bought Louisiana state lands while they were cheap, before the railroad was put through between Vicksburg and Shreveport; and as the road passed near his lands he was thereby made a rich man, as wealth goes in those parts. His good fortune, however, did not swell his head and he remained the same to his friends. He became so useful in his parish that there was never a public gathering of the leading white business men that he was not invited to it, and he was always on the delegations to all the levee or river conventions sent from his parish. He was chosen to such places by white men exclusively; and in his own town he was as safe from wrong or injury, on account of his race or color, as any white man.

After the trains began to run through Rayville, on the Shreveport road, he had occasion to visit the town of Ruston, in another parish some miles in the interior, and as he got off at the depot, a barefoot, poor white boy asked to carry his satchel. Smith was a fine looking mulatto, dressed well, and could have easily been taken for a white man, and the boy might not have known at the time he was a negro. When he arrived at his stopping place he gave the boy such a large coin that he asked permission to take his satchel back to the train on the following day when he was to return. The next day the boy came for the satchel, and they had nearly reached the depot about train time, when they passed a saloon where a crowd of poor whites sat on boxes whittling sticks. The sight of a negro having a white boy carrying his satchel quite enraged them, and after cursing and abusing Smith and the boy, they undertook to kick and assault Smith. Smith defended himself. The result was a shooting affair, in which Smith shot two or three of them and was himself shot. The train rolled up while the fight was in progress, and without inquiring the cause or asking any questions whatever, fully a hundred white men jumped off the train and riddled Smith with bullets. That was the end of it. Nobody was indicted or even arrested for killing an insolent "nigger" that did not keep his place. That is the way the affair was regarded in Ruston. Of course, the people of

Rayville very much regretted it, but they could not do anything, and could not afford to defend the rights of a negro against white men under such circumstances, and the matter dropped.

I have preferred not to mention the numerous ways and many instances in which the rights of negroes are denied in public places, and on the common carriers in the South, under circumstances very humiliating and degrading. Nor have I cared to refer to the barbarous and inhuman prison systems of the South, that are worse than anything the imagination can conceive in a civilized and Christian land, as shown by reports of legislative committees.

If the negro can secure a fair and impartial trial in the courts, and can be secure in his life and liberty and property, so as not to be deprived of them except by due process of law, and can have a voice in the making and administration of the laws, he shall have gone a great way in the South. It is to be hoped that public opinion can be awakened to this extent, and that it may assist him to attain that end.

The Characteristics of the Negro People

by H.T. KEALING

A frank statement of the virtues and failings of the race, indicating very clearly the evils which must be overcome, and the good which must be developed, if success is really to attend the effort to uplift them.

The characteristics of the Negro are of two kinds--the inborn and the inbred. As they reveal themselves to us, this distinction may not be seen, but it exists. Inborn qualities are ineradicable; they belong to the blood; they constitute individuality; they are independent, or nearly so, of time and habitat. Inbred qualities are acquired, and are the result of experience. They may be overcome by a reversal of the process which created them. The fundamental, or inborn, characteristics of the Negro may be found in the African, as well as the American, Negro; but the inbred characteristics of the latter belong to the American life alone.

There is but one human nature, made up of constituent elements the same in all men, and racial or national differences arise from the predominance of one or another element in this or that race. It is a question of proportion. The Negro is not a Caucasian, not a Chinese, not an Indian; though no psychological quality in the one is absent from the other. The same moral sense, called conscience; the same love of harmony in color or in sound; the same pleasure in acquiring knowledge; the same love of truth in word, or of fitness in relation; the same love of respect and approbation; the same vengeful or benevolent feelings; the same appetites, belong to all, but in varying proportions. They form the indicia to a people's mission, and are our best guides to God's purpose in creating us. They constitute the material to be worked on in educating a race, and suggest in every case where the stress of civilization or education should be applied in order to follow the lines of least resistance.

But there are also certain manifestations, the result of training or neglect, which are not inborn. As they are inculcable, so they are eradicable; and it is only by a loose terminology that we apply the term characteristics to them without distinction between them and the inherent traits. In considering the characteristics of the Negro people, therefore, we must not confuse the constitutional with the removable. Studied with sympathy and at first hand, the black man of America will be seen to possess certain predominant idiosyncrasies of which the following form a fair catalogue:

He is intensely religious. True religion is based upon a belief in the supernatural, upon faith and feeling. A people deeply superstitious are apt to be deeply religious, for both rest upon a belief in a spiritual world. Superstition differs from religion in being the untrained and unenlightened gropings of the human soul after the mysteries of the higher life; while the latter, more or less enlightened, "feels after God, if haply," it may find Him. The Negro gives abundant evidence of both phases. The absolute inability of the master, in the days of slavery, while successfully vetoing all other kinds of convocation, to stop the Negro's church meetings, as well as the almost phenomenal influence and growth of his churches since; and his constant referring of every event, adverse or favorable, to the personal ministrations of the Creator, are things unique and persistent. And the master class reposed more faith in their slaves' religion ofttimes than they did in their own. Doubtless much of the reverential feeling that pervades the American home to-day, above that of all other nations, is the result of the Negro mammy's devotion and loyalty to God.

He is imaginative. This is not evinced so much in creative directions as in poetical, musical, combinatory, inventional and what, if coupled with learning, we call literary imagination. Negro eloquence is proverbial. The crudest sermon of the most unlettered slave abounded in tropes and glowing tongue pictures of apocalyptic visions all his own; and, indeed, the poetic quality of his mind is seen in all his natural efforts when the self-consciousness of education does not stand guard. The staid religious muse of Phillis Wheatley and the rollicking, somewhat jibing, verse of Dunbar show it equally, unpremeditated and spontaneous.

I have heard by the hour some ordinary old uneducated Negro tell those inimitable animal stories, brought to literary existence in "Uncle Remus," with such quaint humor, delicious conceit and masterly delineation of plot, character and incident that nothing but the conventional rating of Aesop's Fables could put them in the same class. Then, there are more Negro inventors than the world supposes. This faculty is impossible without a well-ordered imagination held in leash by a good memory and large perception.

He is affectionate and without vindictiveness. He does not nurse even great wrongs. Mercurial as he is, often furiously angry and frequently in murderous mood, he comes nearer not letting the sun go down upon his anger than any other man I know. Like Brutus, he may be compared to the flint which,

"Much enforced, shows a hasty spark,
And straight is cold again."

His affection is not less towards the Caucasian than to his own race. It is not saying too much to remark that the soul of the Negro yearns for the white man's good will and respect; and the old ties of love that subsisted in so many instances in the days of slavery still survive where the ex-slave still lives. The touching case of a Negro Bishop who returned to the State in which he had been a slave, and rode twenty miles to see and alleviate the financial distress of his former master is an exception to numerous other similar cases only in the prominence of the Negro concerned. I know of another case of a man whose tongue seems dipped in hyssop when he begins to tell of the wrongs of his race, and who will not allow anyone to say in his presence that any good came out of slavery, even incidentally; yet he supports the widowed and aged wife of his former master. And, surely, if these two instances are not sufficient to establish the general proposition, none will gainsay the patience, vigilance, loyalty and helpfulness of the Negro slave during the Civil War, and of his good old wife who nursed white children at her breast at a time when all ties save those of affection were ruptured, and when no protection but devoted hearts watched over the "great house," whose head and master was at the front, fighting to perpetuate slavery. Was it stupidity on the Negro's part? Not at all. He was well informed as to the occurrences of the times. A freemasonry kept him posted as well as the whites were themselves on the course of the war and the issue of each battle. Was it fear that kept him at the old home? Not that, either. Many thousands did cross the line to freedom; many other thousands (200,000) fought in the ranks for freedom, but none of them--those who went and those who stayed--those who fought and those who worked,--betrayed a trust, outraged a female, or rebelled against a duty. It was love, the natural wellings of affectionate natures.

He has great endurance, both dispositional and physical. So true is the first that his patience has been the marvel of the world; and, indeed, many, regarding this trait manifested in such an unusual degree, doubted the Negro's courage, till the splendid record of the '60's and the equal, but more recent, record of the '90's, wrote forbearance as the real explanation of an endurance seemingly so at variance with manly spirit.

Of his physical powers, his whole record as a laborer at killing tasks in the most trying climate in America speaks so eloquently that nothing but the statistics of cotton, corn, rice, sugar, railroad ties and felled forests can add to the praise of this burden-bearer of the nation. The census tables here are more romantic and thrilling than figures of rhetoric.

He is courageous. His page in the war record of this country is without blot or blemish. His commanders unite in pronouncing him admirable for courage in the field, commendable for obedience in camp. That he should exhibit such excellent fighting qualities as a soldier, and yet exercise the forbearance that characterizes him as a citizen, is remarkable.

He is cheerful. His ivories are as famous as his songs. That the South is "sunny" is largely due to the brightness his rollicking laugh and unfailing good nature bring to it. Though the mudsill of the labor world, he whistles as he hoes, and no dark broodings or whispered conspirings mar the cheerful acceptance of the load he bears. Against the rubber bumper of his good cheer things that have crushed and maddened others rebound without damage. When one hears the quaint jubilee songs, set to minor cadence, he might suppose them the expressions of a melancholy people. They are not to be so interpreted. Rather are they the expression of an experience, not a nature. Like the subdued voice of a caged bird, these songs are the coinage of an occasion, and not the free note of nature. The slave sang of griefs he was not allowed to discuss, hence his songs. This cheerfulness has enabled the Negro to live and increase under circumstances which, in all other instances, have decimated, if not exterminated, inferior peoples. His plasticity to moulding forces and his resiliency against crushing ones come from a Thalian philosophy, unconscious and unstudied, that extracts Epicurean delights from funeral meats.

The above traits are inborn and fundamental, belonging to the race everywhere, in Africa as well as America. Strict correctness requires, however, that attention be called to the fact that there are tribal differences among African Negroes that amount almost to the national variations of Europe; and these are reflected in American Negroes, who are the descendants of these different tribes. There is as much difference between the Mandingo and the Hottentot, both black, as between the Italian and the German, both white; or between the Bushman and the Zulu, both black, as between the Russian and the Englishman, both white. Scientific exactness, therefore, would require a closer analysis of racial characteristics than an article of this length could give; but, speaking in a large way, it may be said that in whatever outward conformity may come to the race in

America by reason of training or contact, these traits will lie at the base, the very warp and woof of his soul texture.

If, now, we turn to consider his inbred traits, those the result of experience, conditions and environments, we find that they exist mainly as deficiencies and deformities. These have been superimposed upon the native soul endowment. Slavery has been called the Negro's great schoolmaster, because it took him a savage and released him civilized; took him a heathen and released him a Christian; took him an idler and released him a laborer. Undoubtedly it did these things superficially, but one great defect is to be charged against this school--it did not teach him the meaning of home, purity and providence. To do this is the burden of freedom.

The emancipated Negro struggles up to-day against many obstacles, the entailment of a brutal slavery. Leaving out of consideration the many who have already emerged, let us apply our thoughts to the great body of submerged people in the congested districts of city and country who present a real problem, and who must be helped to higher things. We note some of the heritages under which they stagger up into full development:

Shiftlessness. He had no need to devise and plan in bondage. There was no need for an enterprising spirit; consequently, he is lacking in leadership and self-reliance. He is inclined to stay in ruts, and applies himself listlessly to a task, feeling that the directive agency should come from without.

Incontinence. It is not to the point to say that others are, too. Undoubtedly, example has as much to do with this laxity as neglect. We simply record the fact. A slave's value was increased by his prolificacy. Begetting children for the auction block could hardly sanctify family ties. It was not nearly so necessary for a slave to know his father as his owner. Added to the promiscuity encouraged and often forced among this class, was the dreadful license which cast lustful Caucasian eyes upon "likely" Negro women.

Indolence. Most men are, especially in a warm climate: but the Negro acquired more than the natural share, because to him as a bondman laziness was great gain, for he had no pecuniary interest in his own labor. Hence, holidays were more to be desired than whole labor days, and he learned to do as little as he might, be excused as often as he could, and hail Saturday as the oasis in a desert week. He hails it yet. The labor efficiency of the Negro has greatly increased since the emancipation, for self-interest is a factor now. In 1865, each Negro produced two-thirds of a bale of cotton; now he produces an average of one whole bale to the man. But there is still woful waste of productive energy. A calculation showing the comparative productive capacity, man for man, between the Northern[B] and Southern laborer would be very interesting.

Improvidence and Extravagance. He will drop the most important job to go on an excursion or parade with his lodge. He spends large sums on expensive clothing and luxuries, while going without things necessary to a real home. He will cheerfully eat fat bacon and "pone" corn-bread all the week[C] in order to indulge in unlimited soda-water, melon and fish at the end. In the cities he is oftener seen dealing with the pawn-broker than the banker. His house, when furnished at all, is better furnished that that of a white man of equal earning power, but it is on the installment plan. He is loath to buy a house, because he has no taste for responsibility nor faith in himself to manage large concerns; but organs, pianos, clocks, sewing-machines and parlor suits, on time, have no terrors for him. This is because he has been accustomed to think in small numbers. He does not regard the Scotchman's "mickle," because he does not stop to consider that the end is a "muckle." He has amassed, at full valuation, nearly a billion dollars' worth of property, despite this, but this is about one-half of what proper providence would have shown.

Untidiness. Travel through the South and you will be struck with the general misfit and dilapidated appearance of things. Palings are missing from the fences, gates sag on single hinges, houses are unpainted, window panes are broken, yards unkempt and the appearance of a squalor greater than the real is seen on every side. The inside of the house meets the suggestions of the outside. This is a projection of the slave's "quarters" into freedom. The cabin of the slave was, at best, a place to eat and sleep in; there was no thought of the esthetic in such places. A quilt on a plank was a luxury to the tired farm-hand, and paint was nothing to the poor, sun-scorched fellow who sought the house for shade rather than beauty. Habits of personal cleanliness were not inculcated, and even now it is the exception to find a modern bath-room in a Southern home.

Dishonesty. This is the logic, if not the training, of slavery. It is easy for the unrequited toiler in another's field to justify reprisal; hence there arose among the Negroes an amended Commandment which added to "Thou shalt not steal" the clause, "except thou be stolen from." It was no great fault, then, according to this code, to purloin a pig, a sheep, a chicken, or a few potatoes from a master who took all from the slave.

Untruthfulness. This is seen more in innocent and childish exaggeration than in vicious distortion. It is the vice of untutored minds to run to gossip and make miracles of the matter-of-fact. The Negro also tells falsehoods from excess of good nature. He promises to do a piece of work on a certain day, because it is so much easier and pleasanter to say Yes, and stay away, than it is to say No.

Business Unreliability. He does not meet a promise in the way and at the time promised. Not being accustomed to business, he has small conception of the place the promise has in the business world. It is only recently he has begun to deal with banks. He, who has no credit, sees[D] no loss of it in a protested note, especially if he intends to pay it some time. That chain which links one man's obligation to another man's solvency he has not considered. He is really as good and safe a debt-payer when he owes a white man as the latter can have, but the methods of the modern bank, placing a time limit on debts, is his detestation. He much prefers the laissez-faire of the Southern plantation store.

Lack of Initiative. It was the policy of slavery to crush out the combining instinct, and it was well done; for, outside of churches and secret societies, the Negro has done little to increase the social efficiency which can combine many men into an organic whole, subject to the corporate will and direction. He has, however, made some hopeful beginnings.

Suspicion of his own race. He was taught to watch other Negroes and tell all that they did. This was slavery's native detective force to discover incipient insurrection. Each slave learned to distrust his fellow. And added to this is the knowledge one Negro has that no other has had half sufficient experience in business to be a wise counsellor, or a safe steward of another man's funds. Almost all Negroes who have acquired wealth have entrusted its management to white men.

Ignorance. The causes of his ignorance all know. That he has thrown off one-half of it in forty years is a wonderful showing; but a great incubus remains in the other half, and it demands the nation's attention. What the census calls literacy is often very shallow. The cause of this shallowness lies, in part, in the poor character and short duration of Southern schools; in the poverty that snatches the child from school prematurely to work for bread; in the multitude of mushroom colleges and get-smart-quick universities scattered over the South, and in the glamour of a professional education that entices poorly prepared students into special work.

Add to this, too, the commercialism of the age which regards each day in school as a day out of the market. Boys and girls by scores learn the mechanical parts of type-writing and stenography without the basal culture which gives these callings their greatest efficiency. They copy a manuscript, Chinese-like, mistakes and all; they take you phonetically in sense as well as sound, having no reserve to draw upon to interpret a learned allusion or unusual phrase. Thus while prejudice makes it hard to secure a place, auto-deficiency loses many a one that is secured.

We have discussed the leading characteristics of the Negro, his inborn excellencies and inbred defects, candidly and as they are to be seen in the great mass whose place determines the status of the race as a whole. It would, however, be to small purpose if we did not ask what can be done to develop the innate good and correct the bad in a race so puissant and numerous? This mass is not inert; it has great reactionary force, modifying and influencing all about it. The Negro's excellences have entered into American character and life already; so have his weaknesses. He has brought cheer, love, emotion and religion in saving measure to the land. He has given it wealth by his brawn and liberty by his blood. His self-respect, even in abasement, has kept him struggling upward; his confidence in his own future has infected his friends and kept him from nursing despondency or planning anarchy. But he has laid, and does lay, burdens upon the land, too: his ignorance, his low average of morality, his low standards of home, his lack of enterprise, his lack of self-reliance--these must be cured.

Evidently, he is to be "solved" by educational processes. Everyone of his inborn traits must be respected and developed to proper proportion. Excesses and excrescences must not be carelessly dealt with, for they mark the fertility of a soil that raises rank weeds because no gardener has tilled it. His religion must become "ethics touched with feeling"--not a paroxysm, but a principle. His imagination must be given a rudder to guide its sails; and the first fruits of its proper exercise, as seen in a Dunbar, a Chesnutt, a Coleridge-Taylor and a Tanner, must be pedestaled along the Appian Way over which others are to march. His affection must be met with larger love; his patience rewarded with privilege; his courage called to defend the rights of others rather than redress his own wrongs. Thus shall he supplement from within the best efforts of good men without.

To cure the evils entailed upon him by an unhappy past, he must be educated to work with skill, with self-direction, in combination and unremittingly. Industrial education with constant application, is the slogan of his rise from racial pauperism to productive manliness. Not that exceptional minds should not have exceptional opportunities (and they already exist); but that the great majority of awkward and unskilled ones, who must work somehow, somewhere, all the time, shall have their opportunities for training in industrial schools near them and with courses consonant with the lives they are to lead. Let the ninety and nine who must work, either with trained or fumbling hands, have a chance. Train the Negro to accept and carry responsibility by putting it upon him. Train him, more than any schools are now doing, in morals--to speak the truth, to keep a promise, to touch only his own property, to trust the trustworthy among his own race, to risk something in business, to strike out in new lines of endeavor, to buy houses and make homes, to regard beauty as well as utility, to save rather than display. In short, let us subordinate mere knowledge to the work of invigorating the will, energizing productive effort and clarifying moral vision. Let us make safe men rather than vociferous mountebanks; let us put deftness in daily labor above sleight-of-hand tricks, and common sense, well trained, above classical smatterings, which awe the multitude but butter no parsnips.

If we do this, America will have enriched her blood, ennobled her record and shown the world how to deal with its Dark Races without reproach.

Representative American Negroes

By PAUL LAURENCE DUNBAR

An enumeration of some of the noteworthy American Negroes of to-day and yesterday, with some account of their lives and their work. In this paper Mr. Dunbar has turned out his largest and most successful picture of the colored people. It is a noble canvas crowded with heroic figures.

In considering who and what are representative Negroes there are circumstances which compel one to question what is a representative man of the colored race. Some men are born great, some achieve greatness and others lived during the reconstruction period. To have achieved something for the betterment of his race rather than for the aggrandizement of himself, seems to be a man's best title to be called representative. The street corner politician, who through questionable methods or even through skillful manipulation, succeeds in securing the janitorship of the Court House, may be written up in the local papers as "representative," but is he?

I have in mind a young man in Baltimore, Bernard Taylor by name, who to me is more truly representative of the race than half of the "Judges," "Colonels," "Doctors" and "Honorables" whose stock cuts burden the pages of our negro journals week after week. I have said that he is young. Beyond that he is quiet and unobtrusive; but quiet as he is, the worth of his work can be somewhat estimated when it is known that he has set the standard for young men in a city that has the largest colored population in the world.

It is not that as an individual he has ridden to success one enterprise after another. It is not that he has shown capabilities far beyond his years, nor yet that his personal energy will not let him stop at one triumph. The importance of him lies in the fact that his influence upon his fellows is all for good, and in a large community of young Negroes the worth of this cannot be over-estimated. He has taught them that striving is worth while, and by the very force of his example of industry and perseverance, he stands out from the mass. He does not tell how to do things, he does them. Nothing has contributed more to his success than his alertness, and nothing has been more closely followed by his observers, and yet I sometimes wonder when looking at him, how old he must be, how world weary, before the race turns from its worship of the political janitor and says of him, "this is one of our representative men."

This, however, is a matter of values and neither the negro himself, his friends, his enemies, his lauders, nor his critics has grown quite certain in appraising these. The rabid agitator who goes about the land preaching the independence and glory of his race, and by his very mouthings retarding both, the saintly missionary, whose only mission is like that of "Pooh Bah," to be insulted; the man of the cloth who thunders against the sins of the world and from whom honest women draw away their skirts, the man who talks temperance and tipples high-balls--these are not representative, and whatever their station in life, they should be rated at their proper value, for there is a difference between attainment and achievement.

Under the pure light of reason, the ignorant carpet bagger judge is a person and not a personality. The illiterate and inefficient black man, whom circumstance put into Congress, was "a representative" but was not representative. So the peculiar conditions of the days immediately after the war have made it necessary to draw fine distinctions.

When Robert Smalls, a slave, piloted the Confederate ship Planter out of Charleston Harbor under the very guns of the men who were employing him, who owned him, his body, his soul, and the husk of his allegiance, and brought it over to the Union, it is a question which forty years has not settled as to whether he was a hero or a felon, a patriot or a traitor. So much has been said of the old Negro's fidelity to his masters that something different might have been expected of him. But take the singular conditions: the first faint streaks of a long delayed dawn had just begun to illumine the sky and this black pilot with his face turned toward the East had no eye for the darkness behind him. He had no time to analyze his position, the right or wrong of it. He had no opportunity to question whether it was loyalty to a union in which he aspired to citizenship, or disloyalty to his masters of the despised confederacy. It was not a time to argue, it was a time to do; and with rare power of decision, skill of action and with indomitable courage, he steered the good ship Planter past Fort Johnson, past Fort Sumter, past Morris Island, out where the flag, the flag of his hopes and fears floated over the federal fleet. And Robert Smalls had done something, something that made him loved and hated, praised and maligned, revered and despised, but something that made him representative of the best that there is in sturdy Negro manhood.

It may seem a far cry from Robert Smalls, the pilot of the Planter, to Booker T. Washington, Principal of the Institute at Tuskegee, Alabama. But much the same traits of character have made the success of the two men; the knowledge of what to do, the courage to do it, and the following out of a single purpose. They are both pilots, and the waters through which their helms have swung have been equally stormy. The methods of both have been questioned; but singularly neither one has stopped to question himself, but has gone straight on to his goal over the barriers of criticism, malice and distrust. The secret of Mr. Washington's power is organization, and organization after all is only a concentration of force. This concentration only expresses his own personality, in which every trait and quality tend toward one definite end. They say of this man that he is a man of one idea, but that one is a great one and he has merely concentrated all his powers upon it; in other words he has organized himself and gone forth to gather in whatever about him was essential.

Pilot he is, steadfast and unafraid, strong in his own belief,--yes strong enough to make others believe in him. Without doubt or skepticism, himself he has confounded the skeptics.

Less statesmanlike than Douglass, less scholarly than DuBois, less eloquent than the late J.C. Price, he is yet the foremost figure in Negro national life. He is a great educator and a great man, and though one may not always agree with him, one must always respect him. The race has produced no more adroit diplomatist than he. The statement is broad but there is no better proof of it than the fact that while he is our most astute politician, he has succeeded in convincing both himself and the country that he is not in politics. He has none of the qualities of the curb-stone politician. He is bigger, broader, better, and the highest compliment that could be paid him is that through all his ups and downs, with all he has seen of humanity, he has kept his faith and his ideals. While Mr. Washington stands pre-eminent in his race there are other names that must be mentioned with him as co-workers in the education of the world, names that for lack of time can be only mentioned and passed.

W.H. Council, of Normal, Alabama, has been doing at his school a good and great work along the same lines as Tuskegee. R.R. Wright, of the State College of Georgia, "We'se a-risin' Wright," he is called, and by his own life and work for his people he has made true the boyish prophecy which in the old days inspired Whittier's poem. Three decades ago this was his message from the lowly South, "Tell 'em we'se a-risin,'" and by thought, by word, by deed, he has been "Tellin' em so" ever since. The old Southern school has melted into the misty shades of an unregretted past. A new generation, new issues, new conditions, have replaced the old, but the boy who sent that message from the heart of the Southland to the North's heart of hearts has risen, and a martyred President did not blush to call him friend.

So much of the Negro's time has been given to the making of teachers that it is difficult to stop when one has begun enumerating some of those who have stood out more than usually forceful. For my part, there are two more whom I cannot pass over. Kelly Miller, of Howard University, Washington, D.C., is another instructor far above the average. He is a mathematician and a thinker. The world has long been convinced of what the colored man could do in music and in oratory, but it has always been skeptical, when he is to be considered as a student of any exact science. Miller, in his own person, has settled all that. He finished at Johns Hopkins where they will remember him. He is not only a teacher but an author who writes with authority upon his chosen themes, whether he is always known as a Negro writer or not. He is endowed with an accurate, analytical mind, and the most engaging blackness, for which some of us thank God, because there can be no argument as to the source of his mental powers.

Now of the other, William E.B. DuBois, what shall be said? Educator and author, political economist and poet, an Eastern man against a Southern back-ground, he looms up strong, vivid and in bold relief. I say looms advisedly, because, intellectually, there is something so distinctively big about the man. Since the death of the aged Dr. Crummell, we have had no such ripe and finished scholar. Dr. DuBois, Harvard gave him to us, and there he received his Ph.D., impresses one as having reduced all life and all literature to a perfect system. There is about him a fascinating calm of certain power, whether as a searcher after economic facts, under the wing of the University of Pennsylvania, or defying the "powers that be" in a Negro college or leading his pupils along the way of light, one always feels in him this same sense of conscious, restrained, but assured force.

Some years ago in the course of his researches, he took occasion to tell his own people some plain hard truths, and oh, what a howl of protest and denunciation went up from their assembled throats, but it never once disturbed his magnificent calm. He believed what he had said, and not for a single moment did he think of abandoning his position.

He goes at truth as a hard-riding old English squire would take a difficult fence. Let the ditch be beyond if it will.

Dr. DuBois would be the first to disclaim the name of poet but everything outside of his statistical work convicts him. The rhythm of his style, his fancy, his imagery, all bid him bide with those whose souls go singing by a golden way. He has written a number of notable pamphlets and books, the latest of which is "The Soul of the Black Folk," an invaluable contribution to the discussion of the race problem by a man who knows whereof he speaks.

Dr. DuBois is at Atlanta University and has had every opportunity to observe all the phases of America's great question, and I wish I might write at length of his books.

It may be urged that too much time has already been taken up with the educational side of the Negro, but the reasonableness of this must become apparent when one remembers that for the last forty years the most helpful men of the race have come from the ranks of its teachers, and few of those who have finally done any big thing, but have at some time or other held the scepter of authority in a school. They may have changed later and grown, indeed they must have done so, but the fact remains that their poise, their discipline, the impulse for their growth came largely from their work in the school room.

There is perhaps no more notable example of this phase of Negro life than the Hon. Richard Theodore Greener, our present Consul at Vladivostok. He was, I believe, the first of our race to graduate from Harvard and he has always been regarded as one of the most scholarly men who, through the touch of Negro blood, belongs to us. He has been historian, journalist and lecturer, but back of all this he was a teacher; and for years after his graduation he was a distinguished professor at the most famous of all the old Negro colleges. This institution is now a thing of the past, but the men who knew it in its palmy days speak of it still with longing and regret. It is claimed, and from the names and qualities of the men, not without justice, that no school for the higher education of the black man has furnished a finer curriculum or possessed a better equipped or more efficient faculty. Among these, Richard T. Greener was a bright, particular star.

After the passing of the school, Mr. Greener turned to other activities. His highest characteristics were a fearless patience and a hope that buoyed him up through days of doubt and disappointment. Author and editor he was, but he was not satisfied with these. Beyond their scope were higher things that beckoned him. Politics, or perhaps better, political science, allured him, and he applied himself to a course that brought him into intimate contact with the leaders of his country, white and black. A man of wide information, great knowledge and close grasp of events he made himself invaluable to his party and then with his usual patience awaited his reward.

The story of how he came to his own cannot be told without just a shade of bitterness darkening the smile that one must give to it all. The cause for which he had worked triumphed. The men for whom he had striven gained their goal and now, Greener must be recognized, but--

Vladivostok, your dictionary will tell you, is a sea-port in the maritime Province of Siberia, situated on the Golden Horn of Peter the Great. It will tell you also that it is the chief Russian naval station on the Pacific. It is an out of the way place and one who has not the world-circling desire would rather hesitate before setting out thither. It was to this post that Mr. Greener was appointed.

"Exile," his friends did not hesitate to say. "Why didn't the Government make it a sentence instead of veiling it in the guise of an appointment?" asked others sarcastically.

"Will he go?" That was the general question that rose and fell, whispered and thundered about the new appointee, and in the midst of it all, silent and dignified, he kept his council. The next thing Washington knew he was gone. There was a gasp of astonishment and then things settled back into their former state of monotony and Greener was forgotten.

But in the eastern sky, darkness began to arise, the warning flash of danger swept across the heavens, the thunder drum of war began to roll. For a moment the world listened in breathless suspense, the suspense of horror. Louder and louder rose the thunder peal until it drowned every other sound in the ears of the nation, every other sound save the cries and wails of dying women and the shrieks of tortured children. Then France, England, Germany, Japan and America marshalled their forces and swept eastward to save and to avenge. The story of the Boxer uprising has been told, but little has been said of how Vladivostok, "A sea-port in the maritime Province of Siberia," became one of the most important points of communication with the outside world, and its Consul came frequently to be heard from by the State Department. And so Greener after years of patience and toil had come to his own. If the government had wished to get him out of the way, it had reckoned without China.

A new order of things has come into Negro-American politics and this man has become a part of it. It matters not that he began his work under the old regime. So did Judge Gibbs, a man eighty years of age, but he, too, has kept abreast of the times, and although the reminiscences in his delightful autobiography take one back to the hazy days when the land was young and politics a more strenuous thing than it is even now, when there was anarchy in Louisiana and civil war in Arkansas, when one shot first and questioned afterward; yet because his mind is still active, because he has changed his methods with the changing time, because his influence over young men is greatly potent still; he is, in the race, perhaps, the best representative of what the old has brought to the new.

Beside him strong, forceful, commanding, stands the figure of George H. White, whose farewell speech before the Fifty-sixth Congress, when through the disfranchisement of Negroes he was defeated for re-election, stirred the country and fired the hearts of his brothers. He has won his place through honesty, bravery and aggressiveness. He has given something to the nation that the nation needed, and with such men as Pinchback, Lynch, Terrell and others of like ilk, acting in concert, it is but a matter of time when his worth shall induce a repentant people, with a justice builded upon the foundation of its old prejudice, to ask the Negro back to take a hand in the affairs of state.

Add to all this the facts that the Negro has his representatives in the commercial world: McCoy and Granville T. Woods, inventors; in the agricultural world with J.H. Groves, the potato king of Kansas, who last year shipped from his own railway siding seventy-two thousand five hundred bushels of potatoes alone; in the military, with Capt. Charles A. Young, a West Pointer, now stationed at the Presidio; that in medicine, he possesses in Daniel H. Williams, of Chicago, one of the really great surgeons of the country; that Edward H. Morris, a black man, is one of the most brilliant lawyers at the brilliant Cook County bar; that in every walk of life he has men and women who stand for something definite and concrete, and it seems to me that there can be little doubt that the race problem will gradually solve itself.

I have spoken of "men and women," and indeed the women must not be forgotten, for to them the men look for much of the inspiration and impulse that drives them forward to success. Mrs. Mary Church Terrell upon the platform speaking for Negro womanhood and Miss Sarah Brown, her direct opposite, a little woman sitting up in her aerie above a noisy New York street, stand for the very best that there is in our mothers, wives and sisters. The one fully in the public eye, with learning and eloquence, telling the hopes and fears of her kind; the other in suffering and retirement, with her knowledge of the human heart and her gentleness inspiring all who meet her to better and nobler lives. They are both doing their work bravely and grandly. But when the unitiate ask who is "la Petite Reine," we think of the quiet little woman in a New York fifth floor back and are silent.

She is a patron of all our literature and art and we have both. Whether it is a new song by Will Marion Cook or a new book by DuBois or Chestnut, than whom no one has ever told the life of the Negro more accurately and convincingly, she knows it and has a kindly word of praise or encouragement.

In looking over the field for such an article as this, one just begins to realize how many Negroes are representative of something, and now it seems that in closing no better names could be chosen than those of the two Tanners.

From time immemorial, Religion and Art have gone together, but it remained for us to place them in the persons of these two men, in the relation of father and son. Bishop Benj. Tucker Tanner, of the A.M.E. Church, is not only a theologian and a priest, he is a dignified, polished man of the higher world and a poet. He has succeeded because he was prepared for success. As to his writings, he will, perhaps, think most highly of "His Apology For African Methodism;" but some of us, while respecting this, will turn from it to the poems and hymns that have sung themselves out of his gentle heart.

Is it any wonder that his son, Henry O. Tanner, is a poet with the brush or that the French Government has found it out? From the father must have come the man's artistic impulse, and he carried it on and on to a golden fruition. In the Luxembourg gallery hangs his picture, "The Raising of Lazarus." At the Academy of Fine Arts, Philadelphia, I saw his "Annunciation," both a long way from his "Banjo Lesson," and thinking of him I began to wonder whether, in spite of all the industrial tumult, it were not in the field of art, music and literature that the Negro was to make his highest contribution to American civilization. But this is merely a question which time will answer.

All these of whom I have spoken are men who have striven and achieved and the reasons underlying their success are the same that account for the advancement of men of any other race: preparation, perseverance, bravery, patience, honesty and the power to seize the opportunity.

It is a little dark still, but there are warnings of the day and somewhere out of the darkness a bird is singing to the Dawn.

The Negro's Place in American Life at the Present Day

by T. THOMAS FORTUNE

Considering the two hundred and forty-five years of his slavery and the comparatively short time he has enjoyed the opportunities of freedom, his place in American life at the present day is creditable to him and promising for the future.

There can be no healthy growth in the life of a race or a nation without a self-reliant spirit animating the whole body; if it amounts to optimism, devoid of egotism and vanity, so much the better. This spirit necessarily carries with it intense pride of race, or of nation, as the case may be, and ramifies the whole mass, inspiring and shaping its thought and effort, however humble or exalted these may be,--as it takes "all sorts and conditions of men" to make up a social order, instinct with the ambition and the activity which work for "high thinking and right living," of which modern evolution in all directions is the most powerful illustration in history. If pride of ancestry can, happily, be added to pride of race and nation, and these are re-enforced by self-reliance, courage and correct moral living, the possible success of such people may be accepted, without equivocation, as a foregone conclusion. I have found all of these requirements so finely blended in the life and character of no people as that of the Japanese, who are just now emerging from "the double night of ages" into the vivifying sunlight of modern progress.

What is the Negro's place in American life at the present day?

The answer depends entirely upon the point of view. Unfortunately for the Afro-American people, they have no pride of ancestry; in the main, few of them can trace their parentage back four generations; and the "daughter of an hundred earls" of whom there are probably many, is unconscious of her descent, and would profit nothing by it if this were not true. The blood of all the ethnic types that go to make up American citizenship flows in the veins of the Afro-American people, so that of the ten million of them in this country, accounted for by the Federal census, not more than four million are of pure negroid descent, while some four million of them, not accounted for by the Federal census, have escaped into the ranks of the white race, and are re-enforced very largely by such escapements every year. The vitiation of blood has operated irresistibly to weaken that pride of ancestry, which is the foundation-stone of pride of race; so that the Afro-American people have been held together rather by the segregation decreed by law and public opinion than by ties of consanguinity since their manumission and enfranchisement. It is not because they are poor and ignorant and oppressed, as a mass, that there is no such sympathy of thought and unity of effort among them as among Irishmen and Jews the world over, but because the vitiation of blood, beyond the honorable restrictions of law, has destroyed, in large measure, that pride of ancestry upon which pride of race must be builded. In no other logical way can we account for the failure of the Afro-American people to stand together, as other oppressed races do, and have done, for the righting of wrongs against them authorized by the laws of the several states, if not by the Federal Constitution, and sanctioned or tolerated by public opinion. In nothing has this radical defect been more noticeable since the War of the Rebellion than in the uniform failure of the people to sustain such civic organizations as exist and have existed, to test in the courts of law and in the forum of public opinion the validity of organic laws of States intended to deprive them of the civil and political rights guaranteed to them by the Federal Constitution. The two such organizations of this character which have appealed to them are the National Afro-American League, organized in Chicago, in 1890, and the National Afro-American Council, organized in Rochester, New York, out of the League, in 1898. The latter organization still exists, the strongest of its kind, but it has never commanded the sympathy and support of the masses of the people, nor is there, or has there been, substantial agreement and concert of effort among the thoughtful men of the race along these lines. They have been restrained by selfish, personal and petty motives, while the constitutional rights which vitalize their citizenship have been "denied or abridged" by legislation of certain of the States and by public opinion, even as Nero fiddled while Rome burned. If they had been actuated by a strong pride of ancestry and of race, if they had felt that injury to one was injury to all, if they had hung together instead of hanging separately, their place in the civil and political life of the Republic to-day would not be that, largely, of pariahs, with none so poor as to do them honor, but that of equality of right under the law enjoyed by all other alien ethnic forces in our citizenship. They who will not help themselves are usually not helped by others. They who make a loud noise and courageously contend for what is theirs, usually enjoy the respect and confidence of their fellows and get, in the end, what belongs to them, or a reasonable modification of it.

As a consequence of inability to unite in thought and effort for the conservation of their civil and political rights, the Afro-American Negroes and colored people have lost, by fundamental enactments of the old slave-holding States, all of the civil and political rights guaranteed them by the Federal Constitution, in the full enjoyment of which they were from the adoption of the War Amendments up to 1876-7, when they were sacrificed by their Republican allies of the North and West, in the alienation of their State governments, in order to save the Presidency to Mr. Rutherford B. Hayes of Ohio. Their reverses in this matter in the old slave-holding States, coupled with a vast mass of class legislation, modelled on the slave code, have affected the Afro-American people in their civil and political rights in all of the States of the Republic, especially as far as public opinion is concerned. This was inevitable, and follows in every instance in history where a race element of the citizenship is set aside by law or public opinion as separate and distinct from its fellows, with a fixed status or caste.

It will take the Afro-American people fully a century to recover what they lost of civil and political equality under the law in the Southern States, as a result of the re-actionary and bloody movement begun in the Reconstruction period by the Southern whites, and culminating in 1877,--the excesses of the Reconstruction governments, about which so much is said to the discredit of the Negro, being chargeable to the weakness and corruption of Northern carpet-baggers, who were the master and responsible spirits of the time and the situation, rather than to the weakness, the ignorance and venality of their Negro dupes, who, very naturally, followed where they led, as any other grateful people would have done. For, were not these same Northern carpet-baggers the direct representatives of the Government and the Army which crushed the slave power and broke the shackles of the slave? Even so. The Northern carpet-baggers planned and got the plunder, and have it; the Negro got the credit and the odium, and have them yet. It often happens that way in history, that the innocent dupes are made to suffer for the misdeeds and crimes of the guilty.

The recovery of civil and political rights under the Constitution, as "denied or abridged" by the constitutions of the States, more especially those of the old slave holding ones, will be a slow and tedious process, and will come to the individual rather than to the race, as the reward of character and thrift; because, for reasons already stated, it will hardly be possible in the future, as it has not been in the past, to unify the mass of the Afro-American people, in thought and conduct, for a proper contention in the courts and at the ballot-box and in the education of public opinion, to accomplish this purpose. Perhaps there is no other instance in history where everything depended so largely upon the individual, and so little upon the mass of his race, for that development in the religious and civic virtues which makes more surely for an honorable status in any citizenship than constitutions or legislative enactments built upon them.

But even from this point of view, I am disposed to believe that the Negro's civil and political rights are more firmly fixed in law and public opinion than was true at the close of the Reconstruction period, when everything relating to him was unsettled and confused, based in legislative guarantees, subject to approval or disapproval of the dominant public opinion of the several States, and that he will gradually work out his own salvation under the Constitution,--such as Charles Sumner, Thaddeus Stevens, Benjamin F. Butler, Frederick Douglass, and their co-workers, hoped and labored that he might enjoy. He has lost nothing under the fundamental law; such of these restrictions, as apply to him by the law of certain of the States, necessarily apply to white men in like circumstances of ignorance and poverty, and can be overcome, in time, by assiduous courtship of the schoolmaster and the bank cashier. The extent to which the individual members of the race are overcoming the restrictions made a bar to their enjoyment of civil and political rights under the Constitution is gratifying to those who wish the race well and who look beyond the present into the future: while it is disturbing the dreams of those who spend most of their time and thought in abortive efforts to "keep the 'nigger' in his place"--as if any man or race could have a place in the world's thought and effort which he did not make for himself! In our grand Republic, at least, it has been so often demonstrated as to become proverbial, that the door of opportunity shall be closed to no man, and that he shall be allowed to have that place in our national life which he makes for himself. So it is with the Negro now, as an individual. Will it be so with him in the future as a race? To answer that we shall first have to determine that he has a race.

However he may be lacking in pride of ancestry and race, no one can accuse the Negro of lack of pride of Nation and State, and even of county. Indeed, his pride in the Republic and his devotion to it are among the most pathetic phases of his pathetic history, from Jamestown, in 1620, to San Juan Hill, in 1898. He has given everything to the Republic,--his labor and blood and prayers. What has the Republic given him, but blows and rebuffs and criminal ingratitude! And he stands now, ready and eager, to give the Republic all that he has. What does the Republic stand ready and eager to give him? Let the answer come out of the mouth of the future.

It is a fair conclusion that the Negro has a firmer and more assured civil and political status in American life to-day than at the close of the Reconstruction period, paradoxical as this may appear to many, despite the adverse legislation of the old slave-holding States, and the tolerant favor shown such legislation by the Federal Supreme Court, in such opinions as it has delivered, from time to time, upon the subject, since the adoption of the War amendments to the Federal Constitution. Technically, the Negro stands upon equality with all other citizens under this large body of special and class legislation; but, as a matter of fact, it is so framed that the greatest inequality prevails, and was intended to prevail, in the administration of it by the several States chiefly concerned. As long as such legislation by the States specifies, on the face of it, that it shall operate upon all citizens equally, however unequally and unjustly the legislation may be interpreted and administered by the local courts, the Federal Supreme Court has held, time and again, that no hardship was worked, and, if so, that the aggrieved had his recourse in appeal to the higher courts of the State of which he is a citizen,--a recourse at this time precisely like that of carrying coal to New Castle.

Under the circumstances, there is no alternative for the Negro citizen but to work out his salvation under the Constitution, as other citizens have done and are doing. It will be a long and tedious process before the equitable adjustment has been attained, but that does not much matter, as full and fair enjoyment of civil and political rights requires much time and patience and hard labor in any given situation, where two races come together in the same governmental environment; such as is the case of the Negro in America, the Irishman in Ireland, and the Jew everywhere in Europe. It is just as well, perhaps, that the Negro will have to work out his salvation under the Constitution as an individual rather than as a race, as the Jew has done it in Great Britain and as the Irishman will have to do it under the same Empire, as it is and has been the tendency of our law and precedent to subordinate race elements and to exalt the individual citizens as indivisible "parts of one stupendous whole." When this has been accomplished by the law in the case of the Negro, as in the case of other alien ethnic elements of the citizenship, it will be more gradually, but assuredly, accomplished by society at large, the indestructible foundation of which was laid by the reckless and brutal prostitution of black women by white men in the days of slavery, from which a vast army of mulattoes were produced, who have been and are, gradually, by honorable marriage among themselves, changing the alleged "race characteristics and tendencies" of the Negro people. A race element, it is safe and fair to conclude, incapable, like that of the North American Indian, of such a process of elimination and assimilation, will always be a thorn in the flesh of the Republic, in which there is, admittedly, no place for the integrality and growth of a distinct race type. The Afro-American people, for reasons that I have stated, are even now very far from being such a distinct race type, and without further admixture of white and black blood, will continue to be less so to the end of the chapter. It seems to me that this view of the matter has not received the consideration that it deserves at the hands of those who set themselves up as past grand masters in the business of "solving the race problem," and in accurately defining "The Negro's Place in American Life at the Present Day." The negroid type and the Afro-American type are two very distinct types, and the sociologist who confounds them, as is very generally done, is bound to confuse his subject and his audience.

It is a debatable question as to whether the Negro's present industrial position is better or worse than it was, say, at the close of the Reconstruction period. As a mass, I am inclined to the opinion that it is worse, as the laws of the States where he is congregated most numerously are so framed as to favor the employer in every instance, and he does not scruple to get all out of the industrial slave that he can; which is, in the main, vastly more than the slave master got, as the latter was at the expense of housing, feeding, clothing and providing medical service for his chattel, while the former is relieved of this expense and trouble. Prof. W.E.B. DuBois, of Atlanta University, who has made a critical study of the rural Negro of the Southern States, sums up the industrial phase of the matter in the following ("The Souls of Black Folk," pp. 39-40):

"For this much all men know: Despite compromise, war and struggle, the Negro is not free. In the backwoods of the Gulf States, for miles and miles, he may not leave the plantation of his birth; in well-nigh the whole rural South the black farmers are peons, bound by law and custom to an economic slavery, from which the only escape is death or the penitentiary. In the most cultured sections and cities of the South the Negroes are a segregated servile caste, with restricted rights and privileges. Before the courts, both in law and custom, they stand on a different and peculiar basis. Taxation without representation is the rule of their political life. And the result of all this is, and in nature must have been, lawlessness and crime."

It is a dark and gloomy picture, the substitution of industrial for chattel slavery, with none of the legal and selfish restraints upon the employer which surrounded and actuated the master. And this is true of the entire mass of the Afro-American laborers of the Southern States. Out of the mass have arisen a large number of individuals who own and till their own lands. This element is very largely recruited every year, and to this source must we look for the gradual undermining of the industrial slavery of the mass of the people. Here, too, we have a long and tedious process of evolution, but it is nothing new in the history of races circumstanced as the Afro-American people are. That the Negro is destined, however, to be the landlord and master agriculturist of the Southern States is a probability sustained by all the facts in the situation; not the least of which being the tendency of the poor white class and small farmers to abandon agricultural pursuits for those of the factory and the mine, from which the Negro laborer is excluded, partially in the mine and wholly in the factory. The development of mine and factory industries in the Southern States in the past two decades has been one of the most remarkable in industrial history.

In the skilled trades, at the close of the War of the Rebellion, most of the work was done by Negroes educated as artisans in the hard school of slavery, but there has been a steady decline in the number of such laborers, not because of lack of skill, but because trade unionism has gradually taken possession of such employments in the South, and will not allow the Negro to work alongside of the white man. And this is the rule of the trade unions in all parts of the country. It is to be hoped that there may be a gradual broadening of the views of white laborers in this vital matter and a change of attitude by the trade unions that they dominate. Can we reasonably expect this? As matters now stand, it is the individual Negro artisan, often a master contractor, who can work at his trade and give employment to his fellows. Fortunately, there are a great many of these in all parts of the Southern States, and their number is increasing every year, as the result of the rapid growth and high favor of industrial schools, where the trades are taught. A very great deal should be expected from this source, as a Negro contractor stands very nearly on as good footing as a white one in the bidding, when he has established a reputation for reliability. The facts obtained in every Southern city bear out this view of the matter. The individual black man has a fighting chance for success in the skilled trades; and, as he succeeds, will draw the skilled mass after him. The proper solution of the skilled labor problem is strictly within the power of the individual Negro. I believe that he is solving it, and that he will ultimately solve it.

It is, however, in the marvellous building up of a legal, comfortable and happy home life, where none whatever existed at the close of the War of the Rebellion; in the no less stupendous development of the church life, with large and puissant organizations that command the respect and admiration of mankind, and owning splendid church property valued at millions of dollars; in the quenchless thirst of the mass of the people for useful knowledge, displayed at the close of the War of the Rebellion, and abating nothing of its intense keenness since, with the remarkable reduction in the illiteracy of the mass of the people, as is eloquently disclosed by the census reports--it is in these results that no cause for complaint or discouragement can be found. The whole race here stands on improved ground over that it occupied at the close of the War of the Rebellion; albeit, even here, the individual has outstripped the mass of the race, as it was but natural that he should and always will. But, while this is true and gratifying to all those that hope the Afro-American people well, it is also true, and equally gratifying that, as far as the mass is concerned, the home life, the church and the school house have come into the life of the people, in some sort, everywhere, giving the whole race a character and a standing in the estimation of mankind which it did not have at the close of the war, and presaging, logically, unless all signs fail, a development along high and honorable lines in the future; the results from which, I predict, at the end of the ensuing half century, builded upon the foundation already laid, being such as to confound the prophets of evil, who never cease to doubt and shake their heads, asking: "Can any good thing come out of Nazareth?" We have the answer already in the social and home life of the people, which is so vast an improvement over the conditions and the heritage of slavery as to stagger the understanding of those who are informed on the subject, or will take the trouble to inform themselves.

If we have much loose moral living, it is not sanctioned by the mass, wedlock being the rule, and not the exception; if we have a vast volume of illiteracy, we have reduced it by forty per cent. since the war, and the school houses are all full of children eager to learn, and the schools of higher and industrial training cannot accommodate all those who knock at their doors for admission; if we have more than our share of criminality, we have also churches in every hamlet and city, to which a vast majority of the people belong, and which are insistently pointing "the way, the light and the truth" to higher and nobler living.

Mindful, therefore, of the Negro's two hundred and forty-five years of slave education and unrequited toil, and of his thirty years of partial freedom and less than partial opportunity, who shall say that his place in American life at the present day is not all that should be reasonably expected of him, that it is not creditable to him, and that it is not a sufficient augury for better and nobler and higher thinking, striving and building in the future? Social growth is the slowest of all growth. If there be signs of growth, then, there is reasonable hope for a healthy maturity. There are plenty of such signs, and he who runs may read them, if he will.

Made in the USA
Middletown, DE
09 April 2015